The visible word

by Herbert Spencer RDI FSIA
Senior Research Fellow
Readability of Print
Royal College of Art, London

the visible word

Visual Communication Books
Hastings House, Publishers
New York 10016

This is the second edition, revised, of a
report prepared as part of a programme of
research into the readability of print in
information publishing, sponsored by the
International Publishing Corporation, and
first published in June 1968 in a
restricted edition by the Royal College of Art,
London

First edition © 1968 Royal College of Art
second edition, revised, © 1969
Royal College of Art

Visual Communication Books
Hastings House, Publishers
New York 10016
SBN 8038-7733-1

Composed on the IBM 72
Text in 11 pt Press Roman Medium, 2 point leaded
Bibliography in 8pt Univers Light and Medium
Restricted Book Club edition printed in the U.S.
Order number 539

Contents

Introduction

Figures in parentheses
refer to the bibliography

Legibility research in printing is concerned with the efficiency of the visible word. So, too, is the practice of typographical design. During the past century both researchers and designers have put forward proposals for making printed letters communicate more efficiently. This report describes and illustrates some of the more significant of these proposals.

The history of legibility research spans a period of over 150 years - a period during which the techniques of printing have changed fundamentally and other media have emerged powerfully to challenge the supremacy once enjoyed by the printed word as a means of mass communication.

Objective research has produced few dramatic results but it has provided a wealth of information about factors in typography which contribute to greater reading efficiency, and it has confirmed the validity of many established typographic conventions, but not of all. It has shown that comprehension of the printed word can be greatly accelerated by typography which reflects proper understanding of how the human eye and brain function in reading, and which avoids practices that impede accurate perception. There is no doubt that the legibility of conventional printing could generally be improved if designers and printers would heed the findings of the researchers.

Yet, despite the fact that in many respects they share a common objective, there has until now been remarkably little collaboration between the researchers and the producers of print. Many designers and printers remain ignorant of the results of research or view the whole notion of legibility research with suspicion. The problems of methodology and definition, which have greatly exercised researchers, have tended to obscure the significance for the designer of many results. The value of much research has also been diminished by the failure of researchers to define the nature of the printed message, to distinguish between different printing techniques or select appropriate and relevant typographic material for their tests, to consult those with professional knowledge and experience of printing and typography, and to publish their results where they might reasonably be read by those who are in a position to implement their findings.

Some typographical designers and printers shun legibility research because they regard it as a threat to their freedom of action. But typography is a means to an end and not an end in itself, and it is, therefore, an activity which is necessarily subject to certain restraints. By defining those constraints which have relevance today legibility research is likely to provide the designer with greater rather than less real freedom - releasing him from many of his present inhibitions, enabling him to avoid fruitless innovation, and directing his attention and energies into more fertile fields of exploration. By knowing clearly what diminishes legibility, the designer can avoid such factors in those kinds of printing in which functional efficiency and speed of reading and comprehension are of over-riding importance, and in other areas of printing, such as advertising, where typographic allusion and congeniality are legitimate considerations, he can rationally determine how far reading efficiency should be reduced for the sake of providing initial impact, visual stimulus, or 'atmosphere'.

Printing is a method of multiplying a visual message, composed of words or symbols or pictures, so that many people, widely dispersed and without special equipment, can read it, either in whole or in part, simultaneously or at any time of their own choosing.

For several hundred years printing provided the only effective means by which one man, the author, could convey his ideas to large numbers of other men, the readers, in other places. Today this is no longer so. Television, film, radio, magnetic tape, are among other methods of recording and broadcasting what man chooses to express, and it is in relation to these alternative methods of communication and to the demands and opportunities of a highly industrialized society that the efficiency and economy of printing as a means of distributing ideas and information must today be measured. And, further, printing in its conventional meaning, is now only one of a number of techniques by which the visible message may be multiplied.

The invention of printing provided a potent weapon for attacking ignorance and superstition. It made literacy and universal education a practical and an economic proposition. For several centuries the printed book was viewed as an object of respect and inspiration by those who strove towards a more enlightened society. The library became both the font and the manifestation of civilization. It may perhaps seem ironical that the power of the printed word should be challenged in the very century in which the long battle against illiteracy has been won in almost every industrialized country. That this has happened, however, is not fortuitous. The real threat to the survival of the printed word comes not from other, alternative communication media but from the torrent of paper and ink which is today pouring from the presses.

As it has rolled down the centuries, Gutenberg's paper snowball has become an avalanche which now threatens to overwhelm us. Printing in this respect is like the motor car: both are fundamentally efficient means of transport - the one of ideas and information, the other of people and goods. But they are efficient only until such time as production grossly outstrips the capacity of our society to absorb and utilize what is produced. And the capacity of our society usefully to absorb either is not to be gauged by the crude economics of the market place. No matter how great the author's wisdom or how vital the message or how remarkable the printer's skill, unread print is merely a lot of paper and a little ink. The true economics of printing must be measured by how much is read and understood and not by how much is produced.

Printing today serves many purposes and many masters. It appears in many guises. It may seek to 'entertain or beguile or seduce or impress' (227) the reader, to fill his leisure or empty his pockets, to provide him with knowledge vital to his education or information necessary to his work or interests. But, very broadly, the aim of all printing today may be said to achieve one or more of these three ends: to entertain, to persuade, or to inform.

Mass-literacy and greater leisure have created a demand for vast quantities of recreational printing, for novels and stories, for books and paperbacks of all kinds, and for popular magazines of great variety.

Persuasive printing is the lubricant of our mass-production society and considerable resources of technological and creative skill have been harnessed by the advertising and printing industries to the task of producing it in ever-growing volume and variety.

But great as has recently been the growth of printing in these two categories, the truly phenomenal increase during the past twenty years has been in the field of information printing, and in this category, especially, the gulf between the volume of printing produced and the amount read is widening dramatically. The huge output of printed information today is creating a bottle-neck in the evaluation of what is printed. Today, only a small percentage of the material published in professional journals is used. If we add to the enormous effort involved in the production and distribution of such journals, the time consumed by the reader in locating, reading, storing and retrieving the 3 or 4 per cent of information which *is* of relevance to his interests, then it is apparent that in the field of information publishing the basic premise of printing - that the mass-production of the visible word is an economic way of distributing ideas and information - must now be reconsidered in the context of today's needs and opportunities. Personalised publishing - which the computer and new techniques of reproduction now make possible - would eliminate much of the wasted effort and expense which is involved in the current mass-production of information, and would dramatically lower the flood-tide of print.

Photography and the changes in printing techniques which stem from it have removed from typography many of the restrictions and also the inherent discipline of metal-type composition. This newly-acquired freedom from mechanical restriction in typography has served to emphasise the need to discover the reader's true requirements. But as a result of developments in electronics, the human reader is now being joined by the reading machine. The machine, however, reads letter by letter and not, as we do, by words. Yet despite this important difference in reading technique a bridge must be forged between the machine and the human reader if we are to enjoy the full advantages of electronics and to be released from many of the present time-consuming chores of searching, sorting, filing and recovering information vital to our interests.

The rapidly increasing use of television, film and microfilm - soon to be joined by electronic video recording - also requires that legibility research should concern itself not merely with the printed word but with the visible word in *all* media and with the growing need for messages to be designed so that they may be freely converted from one medium to another *over which the originator may have no control.*

If future legibility research is to be of real significance it must, then, concern itself with the realities of the latter twentieth century since no amount of legibility research is alone going to enable our society to digest the current vast outpouring of printed information. The solution to this problem will come from those technical and scientific developments that will enable the wasteful mass-production of information to be eliminated while, at the same time, ensuring that relevant information in a convenient visual form does reach those who desire it, quickly and cheaply. This means that legibility research must be concerned with the requirements of machine-reading, cathode ray tube composition, microfilming, electrostatic printing, and electronic video recording as well as with the needs of the human reader and conventional printing processes.

For several hundred years, under the influence of letterpress printing, the appearance of the visible word changed remarkably little; during the next quarter of a century, under the impact of electronics, it will change dramatically. And just as printing gradually evolved its own aesthetic standards which were different from those of calligraphy, so too will the new techniques of visual communication.

9

The norm in lettering today is not, as it once was, the inscriptional letter, nor is it the handwritten letter; it is the printed letter. Tomorrow it will be the photo-electronic letter.

Like language itself, the alphabet - the basic ingredient of the visible word - is not a static thing. For one reason or another over the centuries the form and the variety of our letters have changed. The invention of printing from movable types initially inspired such changes, and more recently the typewriter has influenced the shapes of our letters as well as layout. Today, with the emergence of new techniques for disseminating the visible word, and with machines joining the ranks of the 'literate', there is an opportunity and a need to review the design of our alphabet and to assess its efficiency. The mass-produced word is no longer merely 'a coloured letter at the bottom of a ditch' (109) but a sign which may be printed, reproduced or projected in a wide variety of ways, and read, under many different conditions, by human readers of widely different education and experience, and by machines. The final technique by which a visible message reaches the reader is, increasingly, outside the control of those who publish information.

'With twenty-five soldiers of lead I have conquered the world', claimed an early seventeenth century author with sublime arrogance and a cheerful disregard for the truth. For we may be sure that while his army of lead still lacked one recruit, it *did* include capitals and lower case letters, numerals, punctuation marks, and other signs. And today, on the Monotype machine, for example, we choose to maintain an army of over 250 characters in order to march into print the words of an author who with less than 90 characters on his typewriter has successfully been able to convey his message to the printer! Today's computer manufacturers might claim, with rather greater justification than our seventeenth century author, that they have conquered the world with just two soldiers: 1 and 0!

dog　cat
Dog　Cat
DOG　CAT
Dog　Cat
dog　cat

Modern commerce would be impossible using Roman numerals. We need now to investigate whether the Roman alphabet in its present form is the best vehicle that can be devised for conveying the information which is vital to modern technology.

Our present alphabet is both extravagant and inadequate. We use alternative forms to represent the same letter so that without even resorting to italics a simple word such as 'cat' or 'dog' may be given in five ways.

Yet despite this lavish use of signs we attempt in English to represent over 40 phonemes with 26 letters, of which 3 are redundant (90).

10

We force one letter, 'a', to convey seven different sound values, yet we represent the sound of 'i' in twenty-three ways (266). Some of the most frequently recurring letters are the most complex and, research has shown, the least legible.

The importance of familiarity as an aid to legibility is often advanced as an argument against any basic reconsideration of our alphabet. But human beings are able quite quickly to familiarise themselves with new signs, and it is perhaps worth recalling the view expressed by Eric Gill in 1931: 'Legibility, in practice, amounts simply to what one is accustomed to. But this is not to say that because we have got used to something demonstrably less legible than something else would be if we could get used to it, we should make no effort to scrap the existing thing. This was done by the Florentines and Romans of the fifteenth century; it requires simply good sense in the originators & good will in the rest of us' (109).

For very many purposes the use of alphabetic language and the visible word is basically an efficient means of communication. We need now to investigate whether better use could not be made of the resources available to us, and the reader's long term convenience better served, by revision and rationalisation of the signs we employ.

In *How to make type readable*, published in 1940, Paterson and Tinker suggested that the evolutionary principle of 'survival of the fittest' applies equally to typefaces. This is an axiom which Sir Peter Medawar has described as 'being wise after the event'. To reap the full benefit, both in terms of reading convenience and of economics, from the impact of electronics on information publishing, it is necessary that we should urgently submit our alphabet to a process of investigation which alone offers us the chance to be wise before the event.

As the following pages show, much research in this century has been concerned with questions of line length, interlinear spacing, margins and other aspects of the use of space in typography, but such research has been largely confined to the problems of continuous text and letterpress printing and relatively little attention has been paid to the more complex requirements of much information publishing. Tests have also usually been limited to measuring existing alternative typefaces, typographical arrangements, or conventions and few attempts have been made to design experiments to evaluate new conceptions objectively.

New technical opportunities now pose new questions about the use of space in the presentation of visible messages. Offset-lithography,

11

the greater flexibility of photocomposing machines, and the use of sophisticated typewriters (which for some purposes enable the author to become his own 'compositor'), provide new possibilities in the disposition of letters and words and in the layout of information. These and other new techniques facilitate the arrangement of words with visual logic rather than as continuous prose, and provide opportunities for giving (and requesting) information with greater clarity. Spatial arrangements, as well as other factors, which have been established as optimum for the printed page held in the hand need now to be reconsidered in relation to images projected on to a television screen or microfilm viewer.

The growing use of 'abbreviated language', of contractions and other space saving devices, which enable the density of information to be increased and its bulk reduced, ought also to be rationalised on the basis of objective research.

The multi-media system of communication which is now emerging has far-reaching implications for the visible word. It is a development which is drastically changing the form of all visual language, and it provides a unique opportunity to reconsider our present use of alphabetic signs and to develop a more flexible and more precise vehicle for transporting the ideas and information which are vital to a literate and highly-industrialised society. This is a challenge which the ad hoc solutions devised by engineers in response to urgent isolated technical problems temporarily obscure but cannot answer.

The development of OCR-B has demonstrated the advantages of co-operation between different disciplines. Only through collaboration of this kind, extended to embrace designers, technicians, perception psychologists, linguists, engineers, and representatives of many other professions shall we arrive at solutions that will enable us to take the fullest advantage of all media in our future use of the visible word.

Investigating legibility

One of the earliest recorded tests of legibility is an experiment conducted by Anisson in Paris during the 1790's. Anisson, who was head of the Imprimerie Nationale, printed two single-page specimens, one in Didot's modern Roman face and the other in Garamond style. Experts were then asked to read the two specimens at various distances until the type became illegible. They found that Garamond 'was readable several stages after Didot's characters had become indistinguishable' (455).

In the historical survey which forms part of his *Report on the Legibility of Print,* published in 1926, Pyke mentions studies made in 1825 by Thomas Hansard and by Charles Babbage two years later (281). It was Babbage, incidentally, who in 1834 produced the idea of analytical engines which in many respects anticipated the basic principles of the modern computer. Babbage, who employed a majority vote to determine 'facility in reading of different shades of paper', favoured a pronounced yellow-tinted paper - 'not a toned paper, but one of an amber colour ' - which he considered less fatiguing to the eye. In order to decide the most readable form in which to present his *Tables of Logarithms,* published in 1827, Babbage also conducted a series of experiments to determine the relative legibility of old style and modern figures (218). He found that figures of uniform height were more legible than figures with ascenders and descenders - a conclusion, indicentally, which has been contradicted by later research (332).

In 1865 Cohn made the first systematic study of myopia, in the course of which he examined over ten thousand schoolchildren, but controlled scientific research into the legibility of print may be said to have begun in 1878 when Professor Emile Javal of the University of Paris sought to establish the relative legibility of letters of the alphabet on the basis of distance tests and visibility under dim lighting. More important, however, was Javal's investigation of eye movements in reading which revealed that the eyes move along a line of print in a series of quick jerks, which he called saccadic movements, and not in a smooth uninterrupted sweep as had previously been believed.

Javal considered that black-letter should be abolished: 'the poor Germans suffer particularly from myopia because of Gothic type, the effects of which worsen from generation to generation'. He condemned excessive spacing in books and periodicals and, like

A line of words in which only the upper half is visible can be read more easily than one in which only the lower half is exposed. Compare the example at the foot of this page with the illustration on the preceding page.

Babbage, he recommended the use of yellow-tinted paper in preference to pure white. It was Javal who demonstrated that a line of words in which only the upper half is visible is read much more easily than one in which only the lower half is exposed (141-3).

Javal's interest in the subject was as an ophthalmologist. His pioneering research has been followed by hundreds of experiments concerned with the legibility of print. Psychologists, oculists, physiologists, lighting engineers, and educationalists, among others, have all conducted studies in this field as well as in other areas of reading research.

Javal's view on the importance of the upper half of the word was supported by the findings of Messmer in 1903 that the dominant letters in a word are normally those which project above the line. Messmer considered that letters with ascenders are usually the dominating ones and play the main role in recognition. He analysed the 'total character of words' as consisting of three main factors: the breadth, the height and the geometrical form of the letters. He grouped letters in four categories: those composed essentially of (1) vertical strokes, (2) curved lines, (3) both vertical strokes and curved lines, and (4) oblique strokes. It is the predominance in any given word of one or other of these categories of letters, Messmer concluded, which gives it its characteristic total appearance. He found that words made up mainly of vertical letters (such as i l m n t) or curved letters (such as c e o s) were less readily perceived than words which contain either a mixture of both or some letters (such as b d p q) which have both vertical strokes and curved lines. He described words containing about an equal number of vertical and curved letters as being 'the most favourable total form' (217).

Letters composed essentially of:
1) vertical strokes: f h i j l m n r t u
2) curved lines: a c e g o s
3) both vertical strokes and curved lines: b d p q
4) oblique strokes: k v w x y z

Goldscheider and Müller found that some letters and combinations of letters were especially important in the recognition of words. These letters they labelled 'determining letters'. Their investigations

for offset litho printing

Pour terminer ce paragraphe, nous répétons successivement cet alinéa en caractères de la **Revue**, en caractères extrêmement grêles et en caractères de M. Motteroz, qui a eu l'excellente idée d'améliorer les caractères modernes en réduisant la longueur des déliés.

Pour terminer ce paragraphe, nous répétons successivement cet alinéa en caractères de la *Revue*, en caractères extrêmement grêles et en caractères de M. Motteroz, qui a eu l'excellente idée d'améliorer les caractères modernes en réduisant la longueur des déliés.

An enlarged specimen of Motteroz's type, right, of which Javal approved and, below right, a specimen, greatly enlarged, of a typeface with reduced descenders published by Javal in 1881 (142). The final example shows the same typeface letter spaced.

Le *Petit Journal* applique depuis quelques jours assez exactement nos propositions quant au raccourcissement des longues inférieures. Informations prises, les types de l'article Thomas Grimm viennent de la fonderie Olive Lazare à Marseille. Malheureusement on a lésiné sur l'approche : l'écart entre les n est inférieur à la largeur de l'n, ce qui fait perdre à ces types une grande partie de leur avantage. Au surplus, l'utilité de la réforme, qui a permis d'employer du huit au lieu de neuf pour le premier Paris du *Petit Journal*, sera bien plus marquée quand on l'étendra au sept et surtout quand on aura recours au six, dont les journaux ne font aucun usage actuellement en France.

Tout ce post-scriptum est imprimé en huit d'Olive Lazare : dans le présent alinéa on a ajouté des papiers minces entre les lettres; je doute que jamais rien d'aussi lisible ait été imprimé en caractères de huit points : on dirait du neuf.

convinced them that consonants are more often determining letters than vowels. They found that while vowels are important as a clue to the number of syllables, consonants 'from their frequent projecting above or below the line, are apt to contribute more than the vowels to the characteristic form of the word' (112).

Zeitler, too, found that 'letters projecting above or below the line were recognised preferably', that vowels and small consonants were misread most often and the long consonants least often (464).

A series of experiments by Cattell in 1885 showed that the eye grasps a whole word as quickly as a single letter (57). Erdmann and Dodge in 1898 strongly supported Cattell's view. They found that subjects recognised words printed in a size of type too small for individual letters to be identified and, on the basis of numerous experiments, they concluded that it is the familiar total form of a word - its length and characteristic shape - rather than its constituent parts, that is important in reading (94). They pointed out that

An inquiry which has just been held at Brighton once more illustrates the kind of leading strings in which local municipalities are kept. An inspector of the local Government Board has been holding a kind of public inquest on the proposal of the Brighton corporation to borrow 55,000*l.* This enterprising public body in its desire to increase the attractions of the great Sussex watering-place has resolved to buy an estate on the inland side of the town to be formed into a public park. The scheme seems to have met with much opposition; but it has been adopted by the corporation, who wish to borrow money to complete the purchase But though the whole sum it requires is not equivalent to

⌐⌐ is not recognized as **5** nor 〈I as **K** and that although the arrangement g has all the elements of a familiar word, and in their

> n
> i
> d
> a
> e
> r

usual order, it is not the recognized visual form. Erdmann and Dodge found that long words, particularly those of characteristic form, were more readily recognized than short ones. Korte, however, found that in peripheral vision short words could more easily be recognized (162). Erdmann and Dodge also demonstrated that perception occurs only during the fixation pauses and that our eyes see little or nothing during the saccadic movement between pauses. Cattell's tests showed that nonsense material is read more slowly than text with meaning.

A new kind of type proposed in the 1880's by Andrew Tuer in which 'the tailed letters, projecting above or below the line, have been docked' to provide maximum type size 'where economy of space is an object - as in the crowded columns of a newspaper' (218). The example on the left is set solid; that on the right is shown with some interlinear space inserted.

An inquiry which has just been held at Brighton once more illustrates the kind of leading strings in which local municipalities are kept. An inspector of the local Government Board has been holding a kind of pub -lic inquest on the proposal of the Brighton Corporation to borrow 55.000*l*. This enterprising public body in its desire to increase the attractions of the great Sussex watering-place has resolved to buy an estate on the inland side of the town to be formed into a public park. The scheme seems to have met with much opposition: but it

17

The results of Pillsbury's tachistoscopic experiments with mis-spelt words, which he reported in 1897, support Cattell's conclusions and show, too, that the reader often sees details which he disregards. In these tests, Pillsbury's subjects frequently reported the wrong or missing letter although perceiving the word correctly. Pillsbury's research also showed that an error in the first part of a word is more easily recognized than an error in the latter part (264, 458).

Huey, like Pillsbury, found that the first half of a word is more important for perception than the latter half (134-5). But Vernon's view that the part of the word that is most important depends upon the particular word seems sounder, especially since the position of the root, usually the most significant part of a word, generally differs in the English language between words of Anglo-Saxon or Latin derivation (431).

The perception of words

The general process of perception consists of stimulation, preparation for a response, and culmination in a response. But although reading follows this pattern it is important to recognise that the reading of words involves processes that are different from perception of other visual objects. And, also, that children perceive words by different methods from those used by mature, adult readers.

Tinker, the most prolific writer on legibility research, has pointed out that the printed page contains no meanings but only symbols which stand for meanings (396). Perception of the written word consists of identification and recognition. The word as written and read derives directly from the spoken word and, as Vernon has emphasised, perception of a word is not completed just by apprehension of its visual and its auditory form of structure. To understand the meaning of the printed word-symbol we must have some appreciation of the experience or idea it connotes. With abstract or complex concepts especially meanings tend to be personal and related to the reader's own experiences. 'To some degree', says Tinker, 'we perceive what we want to perceive' (431). Without the facility accurately to perceive words, comprehension and evaluation - the thinking side of reading - would be impossible. In the mature reader processes of thought directly follow visual perception.

Most adults read at the rate of about 250 to 300 words per minute. As Javal discovered, the belief - still widely held, and echoed in much writing on typographic design - that we read as our eyes sweep smoothly along the printed line, is false. In reality, our eyes move along a line of print in a series of small rapid jerks, but because these

18

Willing

ENAMELLED IRON

ADVTG. CONTRS ON ALL RAILWAYS & STREET STATIONS ENGLAND

& Co

A nineteenth-century London street sign cited by Javal as incorporating the shortened ascenders and descenders he recommended.

movements are so fast no clear vision is possible, and perception occurs only during the fixation pauses which punctuate these jerks. In most situations about 94 per cent of reading time is devoted to fixation pauses and on average, in the ordinary reading of adults, each pause lasts about ¼ second (396).

Sometimes the eyes make a backward movement, called a regression, toward the beginning of the line. Regressive pauses help to correct inadequate perception. Poor readers make more regressions than good readers. Optimal typography causes the reader to make fewer regressions than typography of low legibility. But even mature readers, reading relatively easy text, legibly printed, make quite frequent regressive pauses and the number of regressions increases in relation to the complexity of the printed material.

Eye movement patterns are influenced significantly by the processes of comprehension and assimilation. Fixation and regressive pauses increase in number and duration when the reader encounters difficult ideas, formulae and equations, or unfamiliar words. In analytical reading, regressive pauses are an essential part of the reading process (11, 145).

When the eyes reach the end of one line they make a long movement to the left to the beginning of the next line. This movement is called a return sweep.

The normal reading distance is about 12-14 inches. At this distance the fovea of the retina of the eye, the place of clearest vision, subtends at an angle of approximately 70 minutes. Only about 4 letters of normal size print fall within the zone of maximum clearness, or foveal vision, and beyond it vision fades off gradually. The field of peripheral vision varies from one person to another but accuracy of recognition is usually fairly good about 12-15 letters from the fixation point. Words may be perceived accurately without all the details of the image being at maximum clearness; unclear images to the right of each fixation perform an important role by providing a cue to the meaning of words which subsequent fixations will yield (286).

During a single fixation pause adult readers will sometimes read a sentence containing up to 30 letters but this perceptual span is reduced drastically - to only 3 or 4 letters - if the reader is presented with unrelated letters. Letters grouped to form nonsense syllables permit a perceptual span of about 7 letters and up to 19 letters may be apprehended when unrelated words are grouped together (135, 396).

Perception in normal reading is by word wholes, and recognition of the importance of the total word form has led some writers to assume that only the general word shape or external outline is important in reading perception. But although word shape may make a valuable contribution it is necessary also to recognise that words consist of internal patterns as well as outlines and that details of internal pattern may provide cues which are essential to accurate perception. Tinker has stressed the distinction between 'total word shape', the bare outline of a word, and 'total word structure' (396). The distinction is an important one.

The mechanical skills of reading are important because accurate perception is essential to comprehension - which is the aim of all reading. A person who has mastered the mechanical aspects of reading should be able to comprehend as long and complex a unit in print as in speech. Indeed, the skilled and versatile reader is generally able to comprehend difficult material more readily in the printed than in the spoken form.

The illustrations below show the importance of internal pattern as a cue to perception.

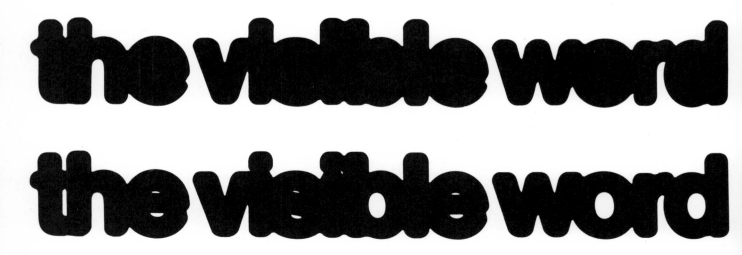

The mature reader has a large bank of 'sight words' - words which he recognises at a glance - and to some extent he also anticipates the words he encounters especially when reading on a subject with which he is familiar. Unfamiliar words, however, can be perceived only through a process of analysis, the extent of which depends upon the degree of unfamiliarity. Word structure may help the reader to perceive words with which he is partially familiar, but is of little value as a cue to the perception of completely unfamiliar words, since such words require that the reader should first identify the sound of the word through careful visual examination of the word details. The verbal context will usually enable the adult reader to infer the meaning of an unfamiliar word but, if it does not, then the reader must turn to a dictionary. To pronounce a word correctly - as we may learn to do in a foreign language, for example - without understanding its meaning, is not perception. 'Perception', Tinker has written, 'implies sensory impression plus meaning' (396) and Pyke, in 1926, emphasised that 'to read means to obtain meaning from written or printed symbols' (281).

Methods of research

The literature of legibility research is rich in discussions concerning methodology. Distance, speed of perception, eye-movement, blink-rate, visual fatigue, peripheral vision, visibility, and rate of work are among the methods which have been used to measure legibility. Tinker (394, 396) and Zachrisson (463) have published detailed descriptions of some of the principal techniques.

Like Anisson in the eighteenth century and Javal in the nineteenth, Roethlein, Dearborn and other researchers during the early years of this century used the distance method for their experiments. This method, which consists of measuring the distance from the eyes at which printed symbols can be accurately perceived, is valid when used to assess the relative legibility of individual symbols or of letters which are intended to be read at a distance (such as road signs, street lettering and car number plates) but is misleading if applied to passages of connected prose designed to be read under normal reading conditions.

In the speed of perception method a tachistoscope is used. This instrument enables the person conducting the experiment to expose a stimulus, which may be a letter or a word, for a very short time - usually about one-tenth of a second - and to measure the time taken by the subject to perceive that stimulus. It allows quantitative observations to be made and is useful for determining the relative legibility of different letters of the alphabet, or of alternative designs for particular letters, or other signs or symbols. But because

21

tachistoscopic perception consists of a single fixation it is far removed from the normal situation in reading continuous text and the results may not be generalised.

The eye-movement method has been used in many experiments and a number of techniques have been employed to record eye movements, ranging from direct observation to more precise and reliable methods of mechanical or electrical control. This method has yielded valuable information concerning factors which contribute to legibility.

Luckiesh and Moss have argued strongly in favour of the blink-rate method of measuring legibility, but Tinker and most other researchers have rejected it as being an unreliable guide to legibility. The method consists basically of counting the number of blinks made by the subject while reading; the assumption being that the reader's blink rate will increase as legibility is reduced (187, 192, 196, 366, 394).

Carmichael and Dearborn made extensive studies to discover whether visual fatigue could be used as a measure of legibility, but they found that no significant changes occurred with prolonged reading (55).

The peripheral vision method measures the horizontal distance from a fixation point at which a sign can be accurately perceived. It has been used to determine the relative legibility of single characters and to compare the legibility of black letters on white with white on black.

In the focal variator method, devised by Weiss, a blurred image is projected on to a ground glass screen and the relative discernibility of letters is determined by measuring the distance at which the image becomes recognizable. Although the apparatus yields precise measurements it has disadvantages similar to the distance and tachistoscopic methods since this method, like those, is different from the normal reading situation (445).

Luckiesh and Moss employed the visibility method to determine the relative visibility of type faces and sizes and to measure the effects of variation in brightness contrast between paper and printed image. In this method, threshold visibility is determined by the use of a visibility meter incorporating filters ranging from light to dark which vary the contrast between image and background (184).

Luckiesh and Moss also experimented with heart-rate as a measure of legibility. They found that heart-rate decreased as the duration and severity of the visual test increased (182).

The haploscope is an instrument for use in studying binocular rivalry which consists of a stereoscope in which two images are placed. It has been used by Zachrisson to investigate ocular preference between serif and sanserif typefaces (463).

Moede introduced motion to compare the legibility of sanserif and serif typefaces (221), but Luckiesh, who experimented with a shaking table in tests in 1938, rejected the method as unsuitable.

Burt has reported that his subjects read faster those typefaces which they found most pleasing aesthetically (47), but most researchers have found little correlation between either the preferences or the opinions of readers and legibility as measured objectively. 'Habit, experience, and the subjective ease of perceiving the text is one thing', says Tinker, 'performance seems to be another'.

The method which has proved generally to be the most satisfactory as a measure of legibility in print is rate of work. This can be assessed in two principal ways: by introducing a time limit and measuring the amount of text read in a given time; or by imposing a work limit and measuring the time taken to read a given amount of material. The rate of work method has been used by many researchers, including Pyke, Paterson and Tinker, Ovink, and Burt. But since comprehension is the objective of all reading, the results obtained by measuring speed of reading are of value only if the factor of comprehension is adequately controlled.

In their extensive series of experiments, Paterson and Tinker developed tests in which, they claimed, comprehension was constant and speed of reading was measured as a single variable. They employed the Chapman-Cook speed of Reading Test, which consists of two equivalent forms each containing 30 items of 30 words each, and, later, a longer modified version of this test devised by Tinker. Each item contains one word that spoils the meaning, and as a check on comprehension the reader has to cross out the offending word. In the following example, taken from the Tinker Speed of Reading Test, the reader is expected to cross out the word 'musicians':

In Ohio there are many coal mines. They are so damp, dark and dirty, and even dangerous at times, that we do not envy the musicians who work in them.

Zachrisson has pointed out that this kind of test puts at a disadvantage the rapid skimmer, who may be far above the punctilious reader in a test of comprehension of essentials (463).

Poulton considers the technique developed by Tinker and Paterson insensitive, because it demands only a minimum level of comprehension, and he advocates rate of comprehension (computed by dividing a score for comprehension by time for reading) as a more reliable criterion of legibility (270).

In areas of research concerned with legibility problems more specific than the reading of continuous text - such as occur in the designing of dictionaries, timetables, telephone directories, bibliographies, or mathematical tables - rate of work may be measured in ways directly related to the reader's task - that is, by simply recording the time a subject takes to look up an entry.

Burt's observation that the results obtained from research often depend very largely on the experimental procedure used, is supported by Tinker's comparison of the results of four studies, using different experimental methods, which sought to establish the order of legibility of ten typefaces. Tinker's analysis revealed that there was little agreement between the results obtained by ranking the typefaces according to visibility, perceptibility, speed of reading, and reader opinions. Other factors in the experimental situation may also influence the findings - including, says Zachrisson, the person conducting the experiment, who 'may be a distractor of importance'. The length of the test period is especially important and many researchers have criticised the short standard time limit (1¾ minutes) adopted by Paterson and Tinker. Burt insists that short tests 'can often be quite uninformative and at times positively misleading'. Tinker, however, maintains that differences which are significant after 1¾ minutes will continue to be so after ten minutes, but he accepts that significant differences may emerge after ten minutes which would not be found during a short reading period.

Some results of research

Children and poor readers may sometimes confuse individual letters, but for mature readers the legibility of ordinary reading matter is seldom impaired by confusion of this kind. However, much early research was concerned with testing the comparative legibility of individual letters.

Cattell (56) ranked the order of distinctness of lower case letters as follows:
d k m q h b p w u l j t v z r o f n a x y e i g c s.
He found that the form of the letters s g c and x made them especially hard to see and that the slim letters f i j l t were constantly mistaken one for the other. He was in favour of abandoning the dot over the letter i and of using a different character for the numeral 1.

Sandford (289) carried out a series of time and distance tests which also showed that some of the least legible letters are those most frequently used. This is most strikingly true of the letter e. Like Cattell, he found that the group of letters most prone to confusion was f i j l t.

Roethlein (285), in 1912, using the distance method for her tests, ranked capital letters in the following order of legibility:
W M L J I A T C V Q P D O Y U F H X G N Z K E R B S
and Luckiesh reported that the relative legibility of sanserif capitals is in this order:
A I J L T MW VX CU KOQ FPY D Z EN R S GH B

In 1928, Tinker summarised research on the legibility of lower case letters (328). He found that there was a large measure of agreement between the various investigations in respect of the following fifteen letters:

d m p q w	high legibility
j r v x y	medium legibility
c e i n l	low legibility

On the other hand, he found little agreement between ten studies concerned with the relative legibility of capital letters. A and L were generally regarded as high in legibility, while B G and Q were found to be often confused with other letters (B with R, G with C and O, Q with O). M was sometimes confused with W.

Tinker's analysis indicates that the legibility of individual letters is diminished by the use of hair lines or of long or heavy serifs. Distinguishing characteristics (as in b d k p g), and a large area of enclosed white space within a letter, are factors which seem greatly to contribute to legibility. Relative legibility is also affected by the size of letters: m and w are intrinsically more legible than i and l.

The 63 different forms used by Ovink for his investigation concerned with the legibility of lower case letters.

Shading helps to differentiate some letters, such as x and z, but a marked contrast between thick and thin strokes does not contribute to legibility.

Vernon found that the ascending letters f and t, and l and t, caused the most common confusion, and that the vowels a and e as well as o and e were also frequently confused (431).

In 1938 Ovink conducted a tachistoscopic investigation at the University of Utrecht using the lower case letters a b c e f g h i j k m q r s t u y in a total of 63 different forms. Each letter had an x-height, without ascenders or descenders, of exactly 5mm and all were of uniform thickness (0.8mm). His experiments indicate which features cause hesitation in recognition and to what extent the basic shape of a letter may be modified without creating confusion. Ovink found, for example, that while the old-style arched a was more legible than ɑ, either form of g g was acceptable provided it was clearly designed according to one principle or the other and that, in the latter form, the 'flag' was extended generously. His tests showed that the dot of the letter i should be large and rather high above the stem but that the shape of the dot is irrelevant, and that, if confusion is to be avoided, the hook at the base of t cannot be omitted or changed to a cross-stroke (238).

Burt's studies, like those of Ovink, show that confusion between individual letters of the alphabet is aggravated by some features in the design of particular typefaces. Burt has commented on the difficulties presented to young children by the peculiarities of the capital C and W, the splayed capital M, and the lower case j in Monotype Plantin; by the lower serif on the capital C in Bodoni and Baskerville and in Caslon italic, which causes it to be mistaken for G; by the barred italic 𝒥 of Baskerville, Caslon, Imprint and Plantin, which is read by many children as 'f'; and the italic *b* of Garamond which tends to be read as 'b'. On the other hand, Burt found that the curling leg of the modern face R, the tail of Q, and the larger eye of the modern e, make for greater legibility (47).

26

Experiments at Johns Hopkins University have shown that some readers have a tendency to confuse F with P,H and B, V with Y, and the numerals 3 and 8.

As well as investigating the comparative legibility of individual letters of the alphabet, much early research was also concerned with establishing the relative legibility of different typefaces, but often the methods of investigation used were unreliable, and the number of subjects too small and the typographic material too disparate to yield results of consequence. In a study published in 1903 Cohn and Rubencamp drew attention to the importance of measuring type in visual, not body, size if valid comparisons of legibility are to be made (65). A great many subsequent experiments have been invalidated by the failure of research workers to recognise this basic requirement.

In his 1926 report, Pyke concluded that differences in typefaces would have to be very radical indeed appreciably to affect legibility under normal reading conditions (281). His view was later supported by Paterson and Tinker who contended that 'typefaces in common use are equally legible under conditions of ordinary reading' (248). Burt, too, found that 'there is, for persons of normal sight, hardly any difference in legibility between the commoner book faces' but he claimed that readers read faster the kind of types they prefer on aesthetic grounds (47). In his research with poor-vision readers, Prince found that differences in legibility between various styles of type diminish as the size of type increases (280).

Tinker's tests, using ten type faces, showed that a sanserif type, Kabel Light, was read as fast as serif types (394). In 1964, Poulton investigated the legibility of three sanserif types (Gill, Univers and Monotype Grotesque 215) and three serif types (Bembo, Baskerville, and Modern Extended No.1). He found no significant difference between the two groups, although Gill was more legible than the other two sanserif faces (59).

Five typefaces of the same body size are here juxtaposed to demonstrate the importance of measuring type in visual, not body, size if valid comparisons of legibility are to be made.

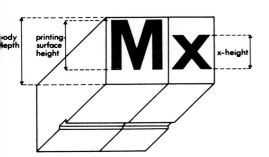

Pages, greatly reduced, from two books
recently designed by Massin, in France,
which attempt through typography to give
a 'voice' to the printed page.

Je les hache très fin

Comment les faites-vous?

Je les cuis dans leur bain

Au four, au gril

Je les fais au gratin

Au sucre, au sel

C'est bien, c'est bien, c'est bien, c'est bien!

C'est bien, c'est bien, c'est bien, c'est bien!

28

The relationship between content and form

During the past fifty years, a number of studies have been made of the relationship, in terms of appropriateness or congeniality, between typefaces and the content of the printed message. Several investigators have attempted to categorize typefaces according to 'atmosphere value'.

In 1920, Anna Berliner published a report on an investigation in which 20 female subjects were asked to rank 18 hand-drawn letterforms, in order of preference, in relation to four commodities (22). Three years later Poffenberger and Franken used the same rank-order method to determine the appropriateness of 29 printing types in relation to five qualities (cheapness, dignity, economy, luxury, strength) and five commodities (267). An investigation conducted by Davis and Smith in 1933 employed 13 types, 23 commodities and 24 categories of 'feeling', and in 1935 Gwendolyn Schiller carried out a further study using the same method and categories as Poffenberger and Franklin, but different typefaces (238).

In 1938, Ovink published his report on an extensive series of tests involving about 70 subjects and 30 book and display types. Ovink elicited judgements on the appropriateness of 13 book types to eight literary subjects, and of the 13 book types and 17 display types to eight advertising themes:
1. force, strength,
2. economy, soberness,
3. luxury, refinement,
4. distinction, dignity,
5. precision, fineness,
6. hygiene, freshness,
7. reliability, solidity,
8. warmth, comfort.
From this investigation, Ovink concluded that in terms of atmosphere-value typefaces can be grouped under three headings: (1) luxury/refinement, (2) economy/precision, and (3) strength (238).

The results of recent experiments by Zachrisson also support the view that readers tend to agree on the correspondence between content and visual form (463).

But a review of press advertisements, in which typographic allusion is often a vital ingredient, published over the past half century suggests that findings on congeniality may have little temporal stability, and such an examination supports Warde's view that the choice of an appropriate typeface is a subconscious act, the effect of which is ephemeral. We may also reflect that sanserif letterforms which have been much used in this century to express the notion of 'modernity', were first revived in the eighteenth century because of their associations with rugged antiquity (224).

Capitals versus lower case

All-capital printing retards speed of reading to a greater extent than any other single typographic factor. Tests reported by Breland & Breland (36), Paterson & Tinker (248, 399), and Starch (305) all show that words set entirely in capitals are read considerably slower than words in lower case. An investigation, reported by Tinker in 1955, involving reading periods of 5, 10 and 20 minutes revealed that all-capital text reduced reading speed by between 9.5 and 19 per cent for the 5 and 10 minute periods and by 13.9 per cent for the full 20 minute period (383).

Text set entirely in capitals occupies about 40-50 per cent more space than text in lower case of the same body size. Eye-movement photography has shown that all-capital printing increases the number of fixation pauses and that, because the text occupies a larger area, the number of words perceived with each fixation is reduced. But van den Bergh, who has argued powerfully in favour of all-capital printing, has produced many examples to show how this style can actually save space, because it allows smaller type sizes to be used (21). Tests concerned with the design of drug labels conducted by Poulton (271) and by Hailstone and Foster (120) show that where very small type sizes approaching the threshold of legibility are employed, capitals are more easily discriminated than lower case.

Since capitals are visually larger than lower case letters and occupy more space, they must be reduced if valid comparisons of the relative legibility of the two styles are to be made. In this illustration, the first two lines show the normal fonts and the third line the capitals reduced to the same x-height as lower case. Line 4, which shows the capital letters reduced to the same alphabet length as the lower case, provides a valid basis for comparison.

abcdefghijklmnopqrstuvwxyz

ABCDEFGHIJKLMNOPQRSTUVWXYZ

ABCDEFGHIJKLMNOPQRSTUVWXYZ

ABCDEFGHIJKLMNOPQRSTUVWXYZ

Bold face types

Paterson and Tinker (248) found that readers preferred faces 'approaching the appearance of bold face type' and Burt (47) advocates a semi-bold old style face as being the most legible for children. Roethlein (285), in 1912, and Luckiesh and Moss (195), in 1940, pronounced in favour of bold face for greater visibility, but Paterson and Tinker's tests revealed no difference in legibility between bold face and normal roman when measured objectively.

Italics

Starch (305), in 1914, and Burt (47), in 1959, found that the use of italics retards reading. Tinker's research, in 1955, showed that while italics slow reading by only a small though statistically significant amount - about 15.5 words per minute - readers do not like italics. 96% of his adult subjects expressed the opinion that they could read roman lower case more easily than italics (383).

Numerals

Studies by Tinker in 1930 showed that old style (or 'hanging') numerals, with ascenders and descenders (1234567890), are easier to perceive at a distance than modern (or 'lining' or 'ranging') numerals (1234567890), but that in the ordinary reading situation groups of numerals in either style are read, in context or in mathematical tables, with equal speed and accuracy. He found that the numerals 3 5 8 and 2 were generally among the least legible and he ranked isolated numerals in this order of legibility:
Modern: 7 4 1 6 9 0 2 3 8 5
Old Style: 7 4 6 0 1 9 3 5 2 8
but arranged in groups the order was:
Modern: 7 1 4 0 2 9 8 5 6 3
Old Style: 8 7 6 1 9 4 0 5 3 2

Soar found that numerals with a height-width ratio of 10:7.5 and a stroke width-to-height ratio of 1:10 were the most readily perceived (300, 301). Berger found that the legibility of numerals improved as their width was increased (17).

Burt found Gill Sans numerals slightly better than those with serifs for short numbers, such as occur in timetables, but less satisfactory for long numbers, as in mathematical tables (47).

Burt considers that modern numerals are easier for children. Many teachers have noted, he reports, that 'hanging' numerals 'occasionally produce an appreciable hesitation, particularly when the figures are grouped' - though much depends, he adds, upon the style and shapes to which the child has been accustomed.

31

Sluis van Ternaaien; links ingang van de ingraving van Coster

trokken de Engelsen echter over het kanaal heen. De Duitsers wilden achter de Belgische kanalen standhouden, om daardoor in staat te zijn — via Noord-Brabant — de verbinding met Zeeland te handhaven, waardoor de geallieerde pogingen, de Schelde te openen, teneinde het vrije gebruik over de onbeschadigde haven van Antwerpen te krijgen, zo goed mogelijk konden worden belet (z Wereldoorlog II).   MAJ. B. KONING

ALBERT-MEER (*Mwoetan Nsige*), in Centraal-Afrika, werd in 1863 door Baker ontdekt, strekt zich in Z.W.–N.O.-richting uit en heeft een oppervlakte van ruim 5300 km², bij een lengte van 150 en een gemiddelde breedte van 30 km. Het ligt op ongeveer 620 m boven de zeespiegel in de grote Oost-Afrikaanse slenk, waarvan de westelijke rand 500 m, de oostelijke rand 300 m boven het meer oprijst. Van het Z. ontvangt het meer door de Semliki water van het Albert-Edward-meer*; in het noordelijk gedeelte stroomt op de rechteroever de Victoria-Nijl (Kivira) uit, de afwatering van het Victoria-Nijanza-meer*. Niet ver van deze plaats treedt de Nijl als Somerset-Nijl of Bahr el-Dsjebel, de latere Witte Nijl, uit het Albert-meer.

ALBERTSTAD is de hoofdplaats van het gelijknamige district der provincie Elisabethstad in Belgisch Kongo. Het is een bevallig gebouwde stad op de westelijke oever van het Tanganjika-meer; eindstation van de spoorlijn Kabalo-Albertstad; hoofdhaven voor de verbinding met Kigoma, Dar-es-Salaam (oostkust van Afrika), alsmede voor de scheepvaart op het Tanganjika-meer. De stad bezit scholen, een gasthuis en een dispensarium.

ALBERTUS of **Albrecht,** aartshertog van Oostenrijk (Neustadt 15 Nov. 1559 – Brussel 13 Juli 1621) en de zesde zoon van keizer Maximiliaan II, werd opgevoed aan het hof van Philips II van Spanje, geheel Spaans en in het strengste Katholicisme; speciaal de Jezuïeten kregen op hem een grote invloed. Zijn zwakke gezondheid en zijn overtuiging brachten hem tot

de geestelijke stand. In 1577 werd hij kardinaal. Van 1581–1595 was hij onderkoning van Portugal (z Portugal, geschiedenis); daarna werd hij door Philips benoemd tot aartsbisschop van Toledo en inquisiteur-generaal. Nog in hetzelfde jaar verzocht de koning hem zijn broer Ernst als landvoogd over de Nederlanden op te volgen. Hij kwam 11 Febr. 1596 te Brussel aan, in gezelschap van Philips Willem van Oranje* en met een leger van 3000 man en heel wat geld. Hij begon dan ook de oorlog met Frankrijk en de Noord. Nederlanden met enig succes, maar was al gauw financieel uitgeput en bewerkte mede hierom de vrede (te Vervins) tussen Hendrik IV en Philips II (z Tachtigjarige Oorlog).

Reeds was toen door den koning besloten de Nederlanden aan zijn dochter Isabella te vermaken, die met Albertus in het huwelijk zou treden (z Nederlanden, geschiedenis). Albertus deelde dit dadelijk na de dood van Philips aan de Staten mee en reisde naar Spanje. Hij werd krachtens pauselijke dispensatie geseculari-

Albertus
Portret door P. P. Rubens
In: Kunsthistorisches Museum te Wenen

seerd, zijn huwelijk werd te Ferrara gesloten en te Valencia ingezegend (18 Apr. 1599), te zamen kwamen de „Aartshertogen" 20 Aug. in de Nederlanden aan. Onderhandelingen over vrede met de Noord. Nederlanden liepen op niets uit. Met grote

The visible word: Some results of research

474   ALBERT-KANAAL — ALBERTUS

SLUIS VAN TERNAAIEN; LINKS INGANG VAN DE INGRAVING VAN COSTER

TROKKEN DE ENGELSEN ECHTER OVER HET KANAAL HEEN • DE DUITSERS WIL-
DEN ACHTER DE BELGISCHE KANALEN STANDHOUDEN, OM DAARDOOR IN
STAAT TE ZIJN — VIA NOORD-BRABANT — DE VERBINDING MET ZEELAND TE
HANDHAVEN, WAARDOOR DE GEALLIEERDE POGINGEN, DE SCHELDE TE OPE-
NEN, TENEINDE HET VRIJE GEBRUIK OVER DE ONBESCHADIGDE HAVEN VAN
ANTWERPEN TE KRIJGEN, ZO GOED MOGELIJK KONDEN WORDEN BELET •
  Z WERELDOORLOG II).   MAJ. B. KONING

ALBERT-MEER (MWOETAN NSIGE), IN CENTRAAL-AFRIKA, WERD IN 1863
DOOR BAKER ONTDEKT, STREKT ZICH IN Z.W.-N.O.-RICHTING UIT EN HEEFT
EEN OPPERVLAKTE VAN RUIM 5300 KM², BIJ EEN LENGTE VAN 150 EN EEN GEMID-
DELDE BREEDTE VAN 30 KM • HET LIGT OP ONGEVEER 620 M BOVEN DE ZEE-
SPIEGEL IN DE GROTE OOST-AFRIKAANSE SLENK, WAARVAN DE WESTELIJKE
RAND 500 M, DE OOSTELIJKE RAND 300 M BOVEN HET MEER OPRIJST • VAN HET
Z. ONTVANGT HET MEER DOOR DE SEMLIKI WATER VAN HET ALBERT-EDWARD-
MEER•; IN HET NOORDELIJKE GEDEELTE STROOMT OP DE RECHTEROEVER DE
VICTORIA-NIJL (KIVIRA) UIT, DE AFWATERING VAN HET VICTORIA-NIJANZA-
MEER• • NIET VER VAN DEZE PLAATS TREEDT DE NIJL ALS SOMERSET-NIJL OF
BAHR EL-DSJEBEL, DE LATERE WITTE NIJL, UIT HET ALBERT-MEER•

ALBERTSTAD IS DE HOOFDPLAATS VAN HET GELIJKNAMIGE DISTRICT DER
PROVINCIE ELISABETHSTAD IN BELGISCH KONGO • HET IS EEN BEVALLIG GE-
BOUWDE STAD OP DE WESTELIJKE OEVER VAN HET TANGANJIKA-MEER; EIND-
STATION VAN DE SPOORLIJN KABALO-ALBERTSTAD; HOOFDHAVEN VOOR DE
VERBINDING MET KIGOMA, DAR-ES-SALAAM (OOSTKUST VAN AFRIKA), ALS-
MEDE VOOR DE SCHEEPVAART OP HET TANGANJIKA-MEER • DE STAD BEZIT
SCHOLEN, EEN GASTHUIS EN EEN DISPENSARIUM •

ALBERTUS OF ALBRECHT, AARTSHERTOG VAN OOSTENRIJK (NEUSTADT 15
NOV. 1559 — BRUSSEL 13 JULI 1621) EN DE ZESDE ZOON VAN KEIZER MAXI-
MILIAAN II, WERD OPGEVOED AAN HET HOF VAN PHILIPS II VAN SPANJE, GE-
HEEL SPAANS EN IN HET STRENGSTE KATHOLICISME; SPECIAAL DE JEZUÏETEN
KREGEN OP HEM EEN GROTE INVLOED • ZIJN ZWAKKE GEZONDHEID EN ZIJN
OVERTUIGING BRACHTEN HEM TOT DE GEESTELIJKE STAND • IN 1577 WERD HIJ
KARDINAAL • VAN 1581—1595 WAS HIJ ONDERKONING VAN PORTUGAL (Z

PORTUGAL, GESCHIEDENIS); DAARNA WERD HIJ DOOR PHILIPS BENOEMD TOT
AARTSBISSCHOP VAN TOLEDO EN INQUISITEUR-GENERAAL. NOG IN HET-
ZELFDE JAAR VERZOCHT DE KONING HEM ZIJN BROER ERNST ALS LANDVOOGD
OVER DE NEDERLANDEN OP TE VOLGEN • HIJ KWAM 11 FEBR. 1596 TE BRUS-
SEL AAN, IN GEZELSCHAP VAN PHILIPS WILLEM VAN ORANJE• EN MET EEN
LEGER VAN 3000 MAN EN
HEEL WAT GELD • HIJ BEGON
DAN OOK DE OORLOG MET
FRANKRIJK EN DE NOORD.
NEDERLANDEN MET ENIG
SUCCES, MAAR WAS AL
GAUW FINANCIEEL UITGE-
PUT EN BEWERKTE MEDE
HIEROM DE VREDE (TE VER-
VINS) TUSSEN HENDRIK IV
EN PHILIPS II (Z TACHTIG-
JARIGE OORLOG) •

REEDS WAS TOEN DOOR
DEN KONING BESLOTEN DE
NEDERLANDEN AAN ZIJN
DOCHTER ISABELLA TE VER-
MAKEN, DIE MET ALBERTUS
IN HET HUWELIJK ZOU TRE-
DEN   (Z NEDERLANDEN,
GESCHIEDENIS) • ALBERTUS
DEELDE DIT DADELIJK NA

ALBERTUS
PORTRET DOOR P. P. RUBENS
IN: KUNSTHISTORISCHES MUSEUM TE WENEN

DE DOOD VAN PHILIPS AAN DE STATEN MEE EN REISDE NAAR SPANJE • HIJ
WERD KRACHTENS PAUSELIJKE DISPENSATIE GESECULARISEERD. ZIJN HUWELIJK
WERD TE FERRARA GESLOTEN EN TE VALENCIA INGEZEGEND (18 APR. 1599). TE
ZAMEN KWAMEN DE „AARTSHERTOGEN" 20 AUG. IN DE NEDERLANDEN AAN •
ONDERHANDELINGEN OVER VREDE MET DE NOORD. NEDERLANDEN LIE-
PEN OP NIETS UIT • MET GROTE

A page from an encyclopedia in its
conventional form and, above, as redesigned
by van den Bergh using all-capital printing.
(The latter occupies less space).

33

Because numerals are perceived almost digit by digit they are more difficult to read than words. Terry found that reading a 7 digit numeral required up to 5 fixation pauses (319-20). But despite the change in reading tempo which numerals impose, tests conducted by Tinker in 1928 showed that arithmetical problems set in Arabic numerals were read faster and with fewer fixations than when the numbers were spelt out in words. Tinker states that the legibility of mathematical tables is improved by grouping numerals in columns by fives or, to a lesser extent, by tens, and that a 1 pica space between columns seems more effective than a rule. In general, he found, the more columns there are in a table the less legible that table becomes (326-8, 332, 381, 392).

Although they are not less visible than Arabic numerals, their unfamiliarity and the complexity of some Roman numerals makes them difficult for the ordinary reader to interpret. Tests reported by Perry in 1952 showed that in all cases Arabic numerals were read significantly faster and more accurately than Roman numerals. For numbers between 1 and 9, Arabic numerals were read fifty per cent faster than Roman; between 50 and 99, Arabic numerals were read almost five times as fast as Roman (262).

In recent years there has been extensive research into the legibility of numerals used in visual displays. Reports in this area of legibility research were summarized by Shurtleff in 1966 (296).

Punctuation marks

Punctuation marks are diverse both in design and application. Some signs perform several functions and the conventional use of a number of signs varies from country to country.

Prince has reported on the difficulty experienced by readers with low-vision in distinguishing between the comma and the full-point (280). Prince considers that these signs need to be considerably

Carl Dair (78) introduced a new sign, which he called a 'fracture', in order to distinguish between broken and compound words.

Fourteen years have passed since the first writing of this book. The interval has been marked by an enormous increase of in terest on the part of both professional and layman in the use of printing type as an active element of communication. This in terest is reflected in the establishment and growth of societies devoted to typography, in the spread of exhibitions and con ferences, and finally in the founding in New York in 1962 of the International Center for the Typographic Arts with a world-wide membership. The literature of typography has also been enormously augmented in this period.

A new punctuation mark, 'un point d'ironie', (above, left) was proposed by the writer, Alcanter de Brahm (1868-1942). A mark serving the same purpose and called an 'interabang' (above, right) has recently been introduced by the American Type Founders Company.

enlarged. This, he has stressed 'is not just reflected in the data and observations in scientific tests, but is voluntarily and persistently commented upon by a large number of both normal- and subnormal-vision subjects used in reading tests'. Prince has recommended that the full point should be 30% and the comma 55% of the height of the lower case o.

It is relevant to recall here Ovink's research in connection with the relative legibility of lower case letters of various designs. He found that while the shape of the dot of i and j were irrelevant, a big, heavy dot greatly contributed to legibility (238).

As a result of his research with the visually handicapped, Prince has also recommended that hyphenation should be avoided.

Type size, line length and leading

Much research has been devoted to trying to establish optimal type size, line length and leading - factors which are inter-related.

The most reliable investigations all show that the commoner type sizes, 9 to 12 point, are of about equal legibility. Larger sizes reduce reading efficiency. Line length may be varied within broad limits without diminishing legibility but research has shown that very short lines slow perception and increase the number and duration of fixation pauses, while very long lines greatly increase the number of regressions. The optimal line length seems to be one which accommodates about ten to twelve words or 60 to 70 characters. Tinker found that while 2 point leading allowed the line length of 8 and 10pt type to be extended without loss of legibility, leading did not make a smaller size of type more legible than a larger size set solid. Burt found that 8, 9 and 10 point Times New Roman set with 4 point leading was less legible than with 1 and 2 point leading.

In their pursuit of optimal type size many researchers seem to have disregarded the influence of reading distance: a 12 point type read at 18 inches is the equivalent of a 10 point type at 15 inches.

Unjustified setting

Lines of type are conventionally forced to a uniform length, or what the printer calls 'justified'. Such 'squared-up' columns of type can be achieved only by varying the space between words or letters from one line to the next and by breaking words frequently. A practical alternative to this arrangement is the use of 'unjustified' setting, in which lines are evenly word-spaced but irregular in length with an uneven right-hand margin - as in this book. With unjustified setting it is unnecessary to break words, names or dimensions at the ends of lines.

35

Blijdorpse ooievaar verkent
op bestelling geleverd nest

*I*n Diergaarde Blijdorp is de laatste weken een man met een unieke hobby, de oud-adjudant van de Rijkspolitie Petter, aan het werk geweest. De heer Petter heeft ooievaarsnesten gebouwd, die elk zo'n 250 kilo wegen. Een ervan is opgesteld in het flamingopark, waar een van de drie paren ooievaars, waarover de Diergaarde beschikt, het reeds verkent. Het was de bedoeling, dat vóór Pasen alle drie de nesten op hun plaats zouden zijn gebracht, maar de sterke wind van de laatste tijd heeft een spaak in het wiel gestoken.

Meer over de unieke hobby van de heer Petter en de plannen met de aankomst van de ooievaars van de Diergaarde op pagina 19.

Morgen Pasen

"Moet je er nu voor de laatste dag een grapje van maken".

Minder druk
dan vorig
jaar Pasen

DEN HAAG — Het valt nogal mee wat de toeristische drukte betreft. De rijkspolitie noemt de drukte op de wegen „heel normaal". Wel is er wat verkeer van west naar oost, dus landgenoten die de zeekant de rug toekeren en het meer in het binnenland gaan zoeken.

Ook binnenkomen van Duitse toeristen valt mee. In de ochtenduren kwamen er aan de grens bij Bergh zo'n vijftien auto's per minuut binnen, daarna liep dit aantal even op tot 20 à 25, maar al gauw liep dit getal weer terug. Het verkeersplein Oudenrijn geeft geen noemenswaardige moeilijkheden.

De algemene indruk is dat het zelfs minder druk is dan vorig jaar.

Ondanks de kou en pessimistische voorspellingen heerste er toch de gebruikelijke Paasdrukte, zowel op Zestienhoven als op de weg.

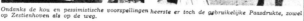

Berghuis wil het uitpraten

Tweespalt in boezem van
ARP duurt voort

Schooljongens
kaapten
politie-auto

Van onze correspondent

UTRECHT —Twee Amsterdamse scholieren van 18 en 19 jaar zijn er gisteren met een surveillancewagen van de Utrechtse politie vandoor gegaan waarin zij waren gezet om naar het hoofdbureau te worden gebracht wegens diefstal van een auto. Toen zij even alleen werden gelaten in de auto, zag een van hen de kans schoon, en reed snel weg in de richting Hilversum. Daar konden zij na een achtervolging, waaraan verschillende surveillancewagens deelnamen, worden klemgereden.

Dreigbrief aan
ambassadeur:
10 maanden geëist

DEN HAAG —Tien maanden met aftrek heeft de officier van justitie bij de Haagse rechtbank geëist tegen de 47-jarige W. S., die ervan wordt beschuldigd de Britse ambassadeur in Nederland met de dood bedreigd te hebben. In de praktijk kwam hij niet verder dan het ingooien van een paar ruiten van de ambassade. De rechtbank stelde S. echter in afwachting van de uitspraak op vrije voeten.

S. kreeg naar zijn mening niet voldoende medewerking van de Britse autoriteiten bij het opsporen van zijn zoontje, dat met zijn vrouw naar Engeland was verdwenen.

Biesheuvel gaat niet
uit weg voor kritiek

Van onze parlementaire redactie.

DEN HAAG — De mogelijkheid is niet uitgesloten dat het moderamen van de Anti-Revolutionaire Partij binnenkort bijeen zal komen om het conflict binnen die partij over de keuze van de VVD als regeringspartner uit te praten. In anti-revolutionaire kring werd gisteravond met een dergelijke bijeenkomst van het dagelijks partijbestuur ernstig rekening gehouden. Verwacht wordt dat partijvoorzitter dr. W. P. Berghuis, die de meningsverschillen binnen de partij woensdagavond tijdens zijn TV-interview zelf naar buiten heeft gebracht, het moderamen kort na pasen bijeen zal roepen

De fractieleider in de Tweede Kamer, mr. B. W. Biesheuvel, die woensdagavond partijvoorzitter Berghuis diens optreden voor de televisie nogal kwalijk nam, ontkende gisteravond tegenover ons dat hij om de vergadering zou hebben gevraagd. Hij sprak ook een bericht van het NTS-journaal tegen, waarin melding was gemaakt dat hij zou overwegen zich uit de praktische politiek terug te trekken als zou blijken dat er binnen de ARP kritiek op hem is als fractieleider en nog meer als formateur. „Stel je voor", zo was zijn commentaar, „dat heb ik beslist niet gezegd".

Mr. Biesheuvel zei, dat hij zijn verklaring van woensdag staande hield, waarin hij de kritiek van de heer Berghuis op de buitensluiting van de PvdA in het formatiegesprek veroordeelde. „De fractievoorzitter in de Tweede Kamer is verantwoordelijk voor het uitdragen van het beleid en niet de partijvoorzitter", zo zei mr. Biesheuvel.

Hij zei het optreden van dr. Berghuis, waarin hij kritiek op de voortgezette pogingen om met de VVD een kabinet te vormen ook gisteravond voor de radio handhaafde, niet ter zake te vinden, maar er verder geen gevolgen aan te willen verbinden.

Zie verder pagina 5

Arnhemse PTT is
17 mille kwijt

Van onze correspondent

In het district Arnhem van de PTT is een bedrag verdwenen van f 17.000. Een van de employés die bij f 17.000. Een van de employees die betrokken is bij het verzenden van geld om de bijkantoren naar het districtskantoor in de Gelderse hoofdstad moet het geld in zijn zak hebben gestoken. De postale recherche stelt een onderzoek in.

Vijf matrozen gewond
door granaat

DEN HELDER —In de marinekazerne Erfprins in Den Helder zijn vijf matrozen licht gewond geraakt, toen ze een naar de slaapzaal meegenomen granaat (vermoedelijk een blindganger uit de tweede wereldoorlog) trachtten te demonteren. Gelukkig ontplofte alleen de aanvuurlading en niet de granaat in zijn geheel. De jongens kregen koperscherven in de benen. Na behandeling in het ziekenhuis werden ze in de ziekenboeg opgenomen.

De Amerikaanse acteur Vince Edwards (38), bekend als Ben Casey op de TV, gaat trouwen met de actrice Linda Foster (22). Het artiestenpaar heeft elkaar ontmoet ten huize van Dean Martin. Het zal het eerste huwelijk voor Linda Foster en het tweede huwelijk van Edwards zijn.

In verband met Pasen zal ons blad maandag niet verschijnen.

Arbeiders leggen werk
in metaalbedrijf
neer na loonkorting

BEEK EN DONK — Ongeveer 150 werknemers van het ruim 200 man tellende fabriek van klinknagels en schroefbouten P. van Thiel en zonen te Beek en Donk zijn gisteren in staking gegaan. Alle machines in de fabriek kwamen tot stilstand. De arbeiders hebben zich de gehele dag in hun werkplaatsen opgehouden, alleen de beambten bleven aan het werk. Alles verliep rustig. De staking wordt dinsdag waarschijnlijk voortgezet.

De kern van het conflict is vermindering van het tot op heden uitgekeerde loon dat de laatste jaren 4 tot 7 gulden per week hoger was dan in de c.a.o. was geregeld. De arbeiders zijn van mening dat het toeslagenbeleid dat als gevolg van het tekort aan personeel enige jaren geleden werd ingevoerd, een wezenlijk onderdeel vormt van het overeengekomen loon waarbij men in het midden laat of de verleende toeslagen al dan niet legaal zijn.

De directie stelt zich echter op het standpunt dat zij als gevolg van de toenemende concurrentie de bakens moet verzetten. Men wil het bedrijf ten spoedigste reorganiseren en waar nodig het personeel inkrimpen.

— EEN DRIEHONDERD meter lange steiger voor zeeschepen op Staten Island in het New Yorkse havengebied is donderdag door brand getroffen. Partijen rubber en levensmiddelen alsmede de overkapping werden een prooi der vlammen. Het enige geladen Noorse vrachtschip Fernfield kon ternauwernood worden weggetrokken. Het kreeg lichte schade. (AP).

WEERBERICHT

Vrij veel wind

Weersverwachting van het KNMI, geldig van zaterdagavond tot zondagavond, opgemaakt om 11.15 uur.

Veranderlijke bewolking met tijdelijk regen, morgen later uit het westen uit opklaringen.

Matige tot krachtige, langs de kust af en toe harde zuidwestelijke wind. Iets lagere temperatuur.

Front page of a Dutch newspaper which recently adopted unjustified setting throughout.

Writing in 1904, T.L.De Vinne dismissed unjustified setting in these words: 'Lines of ragged outline may attract attention to an advertisement or an ephemeral pamphlet, but to the reader this raggedness seems slovenly'. During this century, however, as the reader has become increasingly familiar with unjustified setting through advertisements, printed publicity, and, especially, typewritten documents of every kind, the element of novelty, which perhaps gave unjustified setting the eye-arresting qualities ascribed to it by De Vinne, has evaporated. The appearance of unjustified setting is no longer unfamiliar, and because it offers some practical advantages, permits consistent word spacing and eliminates word breaks, this style of composition is now being adopted for a wide and growing variety of printing - including books, catalogues and reference works, magazines and, recently, newspapers.

Research workers in several countries have recently examined the effect on legibility of unjustified setting. Tests conducted by Zachrisson at The Graphic Institute in Stockholm, which were measured in terms of eye-movements and speed of reading, showed that lines set with an uneven, or 'ragged', right hand edge do not decrease the legibility of the text. Zachrisson used 24 male and 24 female adults in his experiments and he introduced a preliminary reading test to divide his subjects into three groups according to reading skill. He found that, while there were no general differences either in reading time or in number of fixations and regressions between text set with an even or uneven right hand margin, the least proficient readers read unjustified text more quickly than justified text (463).

Zachrisson has also reported on two unpublished experiments, one by Hultgren at The Graphic Institute, Stockholm, in 1954 and the other by Powers at the University of Florida in 1962. Both used speed of reading as the criterion. Hultgren found no significant difference between justified and unjustified setting, but Powers found that his subjects read unjustified lines slightly faster than justified lines, and that many readers failed to notice the difference between the two styles of composition.

Fabrizio, Kaplan, and Teal have reported that speed and level of comprehension tests conducted for the US Office of Naval Research employing 216 subjects between the ages of 17 and 30 gave essentially equal scores for three different styles of right-hand margin: (1) justified, (2) unjustified, and (3) unjustified but with a vertical guide line printed alongside the irregular margin. Reading rate, measured by ocular photography, also showed no significant differences for the three styles of margin (96).

37

3	2	
Tcha,	branch	But
Cha.	of	when
This	his	a
is	studies,	boy
right	that	leaves
enough ;	the	school
but	word	for
he	tea	university
is	is	or
also	a	college,
taught	corruption	he
that	of	learns,
there	the	if
are	Chinese	botany
three	*Tsia*	be
distinct	or	a

Other departures from the conventional style of text setting have been proposed. Millington (218) in 1883 and Huey (134) in 1898 both posed the question of whether a vertical arrangement of words in columns would not prove more efficient. Millington also published a form of boustrophedon, an arrangement which Kujus, in 1955, recommended as reducing eye-movement strain by 25 per cent (163). The proposal made by Kujus, however, was for a modified kind of boustrophedon in which each word still reads from left to right although the lines read alternately from left to right and right to left:

Kujus says this arrangement
fatiguing less prove would

Themerson believes that comprehension would be greatly facilitated by the use of what he calls IVJ, or internal vertical justification (321).

These illustrations, left and right, are from Millingtons book (218), of 1883, which discussed whether either a vertical or boustrophedon arrangement of words would not prove more efficient.

But when a boy leaves school for university or college, he learns, if botany be a branch of his studies, that the word tea is a corruption of the Chinese *Tsia* or *Tcha, Cha*. This is right enough; but he is also taught that there are three distinct species of the tea plant, all belonging to the natural family Ternströmiaceæ, namely *Thea viridis*, or green tea; *Thea Bohea*, which yields the black tea; and *Thea Assamensis*, which gives us the teas of India, including Assam. At most examinations he would run the risk of being plucked, if

The Law Code of Gortyne, still to be seen in its original site in Crete, dates from about 500 BC. It is in boustrophedon.

This page from a booklet presented to members of the Double Crown Club, below, has been rearranged, opposite, by Stefan Themerson according to the principles of IVJ, or internal vertical justification.

It is a well-worn platitude that the purpose of the printed word is to be read. This is a gross understatement. The purpose of all printing, whether of words or of pictures, is to communicate - ideas, information, instructions or emotions. The printed message should be not merely read but understood. Often its purpose is to spark off ideas or activities.

Society will, in the long run, use printing only for those tasks which printing can fulfil more effectively, reliably and economically than other competing mediums of communication.

The present decade is a fascinating and exciting period in printing and publishing. A wide range of technical developments is waiting to be exploited by imaginative printers, designers and authors and bold publishers willing to adopt energetic (and not necessarily conventional) methods of selling and distributing their products. In a century so packed with important developments in science and technology and man's political ideas and social outlook, the book as a tool of civilization has an invaluable function to perform. If all the achievements of scientists, scholars and technologists in this century are not suddenly to collapse like a house of cards, specialists in one field must somehow keep in touch with the thoughts and aims and achievements of other men working in others. Television, films, radio all have an important part to play in answering this challenge. But the book still has unique advantages: it is passive; it is permanent; it is portable. The owner of a book can take what it has to offer wherever and whenever he wishes - and at his own pace. He can consult several books on the same subject at the same time, and so try to arrive at a balanced personal judgment. No other method of communication offers all these advantages. And what is true of the book is equally true of many other kinds of printing. But while it is true that for many purposes the printed word has advantages over other

                    Printers and designers

It is a well-worn platitude that the purpose of the printed word is to be read.
                    This is a gross understatement.

The purpose of all printing, whether of words
                                or of pictures,

     is to communicate - ideas,
                          information,
                          instructions
               or emotions.

The printed message should be not merely read
                                but understood;

     its purpose is to spark off ideas
                     or activities.

Society will, in
                the
                long
                run,
          use printing only for those tasks
                         which printing can fulfil more effectively,
                                              reliably
                                              & economically
                         than other competing mediums
                                                   of
                                                   communi-
                                                   cation.

The present decade is a fascinating
                     & exciting period in printing
                                      & publishing.

A wide range of technical developments
     is waiting to be exploited by imaginative printers,
                                  designers
                                  & authors
                                  & bold publishers willing to adopt
                                                energetic
                                                (and not necessarily conventional)
                                                methods of selling
                                                      & distributing their
                                                                   products.

In a century so packed with important developments in science
                                      & technology
                                      & man's political ideas
                                        & social outlook,
the book as a tool of civilization has an invaluable function to perform.

If all the achievements of scientists,
                          scholars
                          & technologists in this century
               are not suddenly to collapse like a house of cards,
specialists in one field must
                     somehow
                     keep in touch with the thoughts
                                       & aims
                                       & achievements of other men
                                                     working in others.

Television,
     films,
     radio all have an important part to play in answering this challenge.

But
  the book still has unique advantages: it is passive;
                                           it is permanent;
                                           it is portable.

This is   **of the**   **style of**
an example   **square-span**   **presentation**

By comparison with IVJ, the 'square-span' and 'spaced-unit' styles of presentation seem rather less drastic proposals.

This is an example   of the spaced-unit   style of presentation

Reading speed and comprehension tests conducted by North and Jenkins in 1951 showed that their spaced-unit style was superior to both square-span and conventional typography (236). There was no loss in accuracy of retention. A tachistoscopic test carried out by Nahinsky in 1956, however, showed the square-span style to be significantly superior to the other two styles (230).

Dearborn, Johnston & Carmichael have proposed the peak-stress method and they claim that setting in bold the word in a sentence which carries peak stress significantly improves comprehension (81). In a similar vein, Klare, Mabry & Gustafson have proposed what they call 'patterning' - that is, the underlining of certain words in the text (155).

Paragraphs and indention

In *How to Make Type Readable,* published in 1940, Paterson and Tinker wrote: 'It is universal practice to separate 'thought units' mechanically by indenting the first line of every paragraph' (248).

But although indention is a very widely used convention there are of course other ways of indicating the beginning of a paragraph.

One method is to use a paragraph mark. The modern paragraph mark § is derived from the mediaeval sign ¶ which was originally written in colour in the middle of continuous text to mark the beginning of a new section. In the late middle ages it became the practice to begin a new paragraph on a new line and, although retained for some time, the redundant paragraph mark gradually disappeared. But the paragraph mark occasionally re-emerges as, for example, in Eric Gill's *An Essay on Typography* (109), published in 1931, or Geoffrey Dowding's *Factors in the Choice of Type Faces* (89), and it quite often appears, disguised, in advertisements and publicity printing.

Another alternative to paragraph indention, and one frequently encountered today, is the use of extra space to separate paragraphs. This method is employed increasingly in printing and, especially, in typewritten matter of all kinds.

42

Paragraph marks as used by Eric Gill in 1931, right; in a recent press advertisement, below; and by Geoffrey Dowding, below right.

had no eye for good printing or thought of printing as an inferior way of reproducing lettering. It is **not** true that a hand-operated printing press is essentially the same as one automatically fed and operated by what they call 'power', any more than it is true to say that a hand loom is essentially the same kind of machine as a power loom. It is not a proper use of words to call the work of Caxton 'mass' production. and least of all is it true to say that the early printers were simply men of business.

¶ Here we may content ourselves with the follow-ing affirmations: i. The printing press is a tool for making prints better, as well as quicker, than it can be done by pressing with the unaided hand. The press, whether the pressure be applied by means of levers, screws or rollers, is not simply suitable but indispensable. ij. Writing may be all that calligra-phers say of it, & printed lettering is neither better nor worse; it is simply a different kind of thing. Good printing has its own kind of goodness; the motives of its inventors do not concern us. iij. The service ren-dered to the world by printers is best talked about by those who are served. The printer had better confine his attention to the well doing of what he wants to do or is asked to do namely to print. When the ser-

Thursday. The sun was baking this afternoon, but it's beginning to cool off a little now. The sea's still beautifully warm, though. One last swim and we'll go-back to the hotel for a shower and a long, cool drink on the balcony. Talk about what we did this morning. The trip out by car to Salamis to see that fabulous ancient city. And the courteous old man we met with his two donkeys. And shopping for presents in the market. ☐ This evening we'll eat out at that little taverna on the beach. The one with the marvellous sea-food, and music and dancing. And tomorrow, water ski-ing and more hot sun. ☐ This is a marvellous holiday, our Silver Wing Holiday in Cyprus. £91 for two weeks in a luxurious modern hotel with air travel by the smooth jets of OLYMPIC AIRWAYS and BEA. ☐ Send in this coupon for more details. You will receive a 24 page colour Silver Wing brochure on holidays in Cyprus and the Eastern Mediterranean. For full information on Cyprus, contact the Cyprus Trade and Tourist Centre, 213, Regent Street, London, W.1.

Ideally the choice of paper for a particular job follows that of the text type, and in all fine book production this order usually obtains. But the economics of commercial publishing are such that all well-established houses buy their own paper and supply it to their printers. And not only the economics of commercial publishing but the fluctuations in paper supply (due to the exigencies of the times) often make the deliberate choice of particular papers extremely difficult.

⟦In ephemeral work the choice of paper is necessarily determined in advance in certain instances, e.g. in magazine and newspaper produc-tion; and in the wide range of publicity & other business printing the choice of paper is often governed almost entirely by economics, or by convenience, i.e. by what the printer has in stock—especially if the work is required urgently.

⟦But when economics or other factors do not exercise a complete stranglehold on choice the papermakers offer a very wide range of papers—from the many varieties of hand-made to the repulsively smooth and lifeless surface and 'feel' of the so-called 'art' papers. In choosing a paper, its surface, its 'feel', and its colour will be taken into account. The student-typographer should familiarize himself not only with the wide range of printing papers available but also with the effects of printing, by letterpress,[1] the normal composition sizes of various faces on them so that he may be able to judge whether type and paper are suited to each other. Below, the many types of printing papers have been concentrated into five broad groups. It will be seen that while an

Now when Jesus was born in Bethlehem of Judea,
    in the days of Herod the king,
  behold,
there came wise men from the east to Jerusalem,
   saying,
         Where is he that is born King of the Jews?
         for we have seen his star, in the east,
         and are come to worship him.
  When Herod the king had heard these things,
he was troubled, and all Jerusalem with him.
  And when he had gathered all the chief priests and scribes of the people together,
he demanded of them where Christ should be born.
And they said unto him.
     In Bethlehem of Judea:
     for thus it is written by the prophet:

Above: An example of the 'cadenced form' used by Morton C. Bradley for the New Testament produced by The Riverside Press.

In books, magazines, and newspapers, indention is generally one-em of the body size of metal type. This is sometimes increased where wider-than-normal line lengths are used. Only rarely is a book produced with paragraph indention less than 1-em. In advertisement settings indention varies considerably, and in typewritten matter wide indention is common. The Pitman School, for example, teaches typists to indent paragraphs by space equivalent to 5 characters.

Paterson and Tinker expressed the opinion that 'the practice of separating thought units by regular indentation justifies itself in terms of legibility' (248) but they did not consider alternative methods of indicating 'thought units', and their findings are based on test materials which cannot be regarded as typical of the normal paragraph.

The test materials adopted by Paterson and Tinker for other legibility studies had originally been set up as thirty numbered paragraphs of thirty words each. But such a series of brief thought units gave the page an unfamiliar appearance and made it difficult to investigate such factors as leading and line width. They decided, therefore, to have the material reset as five paragraphs each containing six (numbered) 'thought units'. These two contrasting arrangements were then used to test 180 college students and the results showed that the page containing five paragraphs was read 7.3 per cent more slowly than the alternative, thirty paragraph, arrangement. Paterson and Tinker concluded that this result justifies *indention*, but it would, perhaps, be more reasonable to regard this result simply as confirming what one would expect - that unrelated 'thought units' are more difficult to read if strung together in a single paragraph than if set out separately, as logic demands.

Dearborn (79), in 1906, and Huey (135), in 1908, suggested that legibility of text might be improved by slightly indenting alternate lines. In 1917, in a series of experiments for the New York City Telephone Company designed to improve the legibility of telephone directories, Baird tested the effect of indenting every other line. He found that this method increased the speed and accuracy of locating telephone numbers by about 5 per cent, but that increased leading had greater advantage (7). Later experiments conducted by Paterson and Tinker, involving 538 readers, showed that indenting alternate lines slowed reading by 3.4 per cent compared with regular printing in which all lines, except the first of each paragraph, are ranged left (248).

Margins

The conventional margins used in books reduce the printed area to approximately half the total page area. Paterson and Tinker measured 400 text books and found that, while the area devoted to margins varied from as much as 71 per cent in some books to as little as 24 per cent in others, margins occupied more than 44% of the total page in 77.5 per cent of the books examined, and that the average area devoted to text was 52.8 per cent (248). Economy regulations introduced in Britain during the second world war required that the type area should fill at least 58% of the page.

The traditional margins favoured in formal book work are in a ratio of 1 (inner margin), 1½ (head), 2 (foredge), 2½ (foot), or 1½, 2, 3, 4 (144, 314). Many book designers insist that margins of this order are desirable on aesthetic grounds since the unit of a book is not a single page but a double-spread, and because the optical centre of a page is higher than the true centre. Similarly, because of a 'part-whole proportion illusion', an area of typematter occupying only 50% of the total page area will seem to be much larger. Paterson and Tinker have reported on a test conducted in this connection by Dorothy Plain (246, 248). Using white cards with black centre areas she obtained estimates of the proportions of centre areas to total card areas from 300 subjects. She found that her subjects over-estimated the size of the centre area by an average of 18 per cent.

Writing in 1881, one of the earliest authorities on legibility, Weber, insisted that margins are unnecessary (438). But other writers, including Cohn, Dearborn, and Burt, have argued strongly in favour of margins, claiming, among other things, that they help to keep out peripheral colour stimuli and prevent the eye in the backward movement from swinging off the page. Burt gives no evidence to support his view that 'books with excessively narrow margins are more apt to produce visual fatigue'.

Paterson and Tinker conducted reading speed tests involving 190 readers and using material printed in 10pt Scotch Roman, 2 point leaded, set to a line width of 19 picas. They compared material printed with 7/8 inch margins, left and right, with material printed 'without margins' (actually a 1/16 inch margin was used).

Gay graffiti on a dark slum wall, vigorous decoration abruptly exposed in a half-demolished house, strange juxtapositions revealed through the sad ribbons of torn posters, an old tin box pressed into service as a primitive shrine, the peat cutter's serrated trail, a rough stone wall riding over a barren landscape – such things are more than fleeting curiosities. Each of them proclaims, for those with eyes to see, some significant truth about the life and the people of that region, about man's combat with nature, his fellows and his conscience. In noisy cities and in quiet villages, in busy streets and sleeping fields one is surrounded by evidence of man's restless energy, his faith and beliefs, his moods of hope and despair, his conflicting creative and destructive urges, his wit, his frustrations, his meanness and his magnanimity, his inconsistency, and his mortality.

Gay graffiti on a dark slum wall, vigorous decoration abruptly exposed in a half-demolished house, strange juxtapositions revealed through the sad ribbons of torn posters, an old tin box pressed into service as a primitive shrine, the peat cutter's serrated trail, a rough stone wall riding over a barren landscape – such things are more than fleeting curiosities. Each of them proclaims, for those with eyes to see, some significant truth about the life and the people of that region, about man's combat with nature, his fellows and his conscience. In noisy cities and in quiet villages, in busy streets and sleeping fields one is surrounded by evidence of man's restless energy, his faith and beliefs, his moods of hope and despair, his conflicting creative and destructive urges, his wit, his frustrations, his meanness and his magnanimity, his inconsistency, and his mortality.

The effect of reading angle on the visual
size of type. The text, opposite, reproduced
at an angle of 90° to the line of vision, is
shown above at a 135° angle.

Surprisingly, margins yielded no advantage - indeed, the material printed without margins was read slightly, though not significantly, faster (1.9 per cent).

On the basis of these tests, Paterson and Tinker concluded that 'since margins are not essential from the point of view of legibility, and since they add greatly to costs, it is clear that they must be justified, if justified at all, solely in terms of aesthetics' (248). In a 'Tabular Summary of Typography Recommendations', the authors propose that ¼ inch for head, outer, and foot margins and ¾ inch for the inner margin would provide a satisfactory printing arrangement. (Their convictions and recommendations are, however, conveyed to the reader on pages printed with more generous margins than these and following, the preface explains, 'specifications for an ideal printed page' drawn up by the authors!).

Paterson and Tinker's conclusion ignores the practical functions of margins quite apart from considerations of legibility or aesthetics: margins provide space for making notes and for the fingers to hold the book without obscuring any part of the printed text or image (and it is for this latter reason that the outer and foot margins are conventionally wider than the inner and head margins).

The tests used by Paterson and Tinker were, as usual, of short duration - 1¾ minutes - and it seems probable that longer tests would, in this case, yield a different result. As a guide to efficient margins for a book consisting of continuous text, Paterson and Tinker's tests must, therefore, be regarded as inadequate, but the results of their short tests are of significance in relation to many kinds of information publishing, where the reader will often be concerned only with brief passages of text. Paterson and Tinker's results seem reliably to demonstrate that for such short passages of text - up to, say, 500 words (the amount normally read in 1¾ minutes) - very narrow margins do not diminish legibility.

Page size

Page size seems generally to be determined by either economic or aesthetic considerations. Yet there is a relationship between page size and legibility since the physical factors of size and weight may influence the distance and angle at which a publication is read. A flimsy publication in a very large format, such as a newspaper, may compel the reader to bend or fold the page. A large and heavy book which cannot comfortably be supported in the hands will, if placed flat on a table, be read at a more acute angle to the reader's line of vision than a smaller book held in the hand. Any departure from the 90° angle will diminish the optical size of the type: a 12 point type read at a 135° angle becomes, in effect, approximately 8 point.

Gay graffiti on a dark slum wall, vigorous decoration abruptly exposed in a half-demolished house, strange juxtapositions revealed through the sad ribbons of torn posters, an old tin box pressed into service as a primitive shrine, the peat cutter's serrated trail, a rough stone wall riding over a barren landscape – such things are more than fleeting curiosities. Each of them proclaims, for those with eyes to see, some significant truth about the life and the people of that region, about man's combat with nature, his fellows and his conscience. In noisy cities and in quiet villages, in busy streets and sleeping fields one is surrounded by evidence of man's restless energy, his faith and beliefs, his moods of hope and despair, his conflicting creative and destructive urges, his wit, his frustrations, his meanness and his magnanimity, his inconsistency, and his mortality.

This photograph of the text reproduced on page 46 shows the distortions which occur when the page is slightly curved.

A nineteenth-century view (218) of the effect of vibration on reading:
'A fertile source of injury to the sight is the practice, become almost universal, of reading in railway carriages. This is more especially the case when the nature and amount of light is constantly changing, as for instance on the metropolitan railways, where in some portions of the route the train plunges incessantly into daylight and out again. The eyes are called upon by the ever-varying intensity of the light, for a continual new adjustment of the focus of vision, which, added to the muscular tension necessitated by the vibration of the carriage, will sufficiently account for much of the nervous malaise felt by some habitual travellers on these lines.'

xiv: Introduction:

contestably more idiotic, although scarcely so idiomatic as "Croquer le marmot" and "Graisser la patte."

The column in Portuguese which runs throughout the original work is omitted, and only a sufficient number of the English extracts are culled to enable the reader to form a just idea of the unintentionally humorous style that an author may fall into who attempts to follow the intricacies of "English as she is spoke" by the aid of a French dictionary and a phrase-book.

It is to be trusted the eccentric "Guide" to which this short sketch is intended to serve as Introduction —and, so far as may be, elucidation—is not a fair specimen of Portuguese or Brazilian educational literature; if such be the case the schoolmaster is indeed

A MILE A MINUTE !
OR,
How it looks in a Railway Carriage.

A survey by Paterson and Tinker of 1000 text books and 500 American and foreign journals, published in 1940, revealed that nearly 90% of the text books were 8 x 5 inches or smaller, but that journals were produced in a wide range of sizes from 7 x 4 inches up to 14 x 11 inches (248). Paterson and Tinker commented 'It almost looks as though the size of page is a matter of whim' and went on to recommend that printers, publishers, and paper makers should arrive at an agreement on page sizes 'that would minimize the waste of paper stock that must now occur'.

It is probable that a survey similar to Paterson and Tinker's, if conducted today, would reveal larger average page sizes, and perhaps still wider diversity in both text books and journals than in 1940. However, the gradual adoption of International Paper Sizes (ISO) by publishers and industries in many countries during recent years is at last beginning to bring some discipline to the size of publications.

Non-horizontal alignment

Text which departs from the normal horizontal alignment complicates the oculomotor adjustments in reading by imposing unusual demands upon the eye muscles during the saccadic movements between fixation pauses. It reduces the reader's ability effectively to utilise peripheral vision. Obliquely arranged lines are more difficult to read than those which run vertically upwards or downwards, as on the spines of books (385, 394).

50

Tests conducted by Gould, Raines and Ruckmick (113) and by Tinker produced no evidence that titles on spines arranged from head to foot were more legible than those which ran upwards.

Paper and ink

Prince has stated that, because it provides the greatest contrast between background and image, maximum paper reflectance promotes maximum reading efficiency. He has also pointed out that opacity is important and that the reflectance of a paper can, for example, be reduced from 82 per cent when stacked to 76 per cent when printed on both sides of the sheet (280).

Two experiments conducted by Paterson and Tinker showed that a flint enamel with over 95 per cent glare retarded reading by a small but significant amount, but that with well diffused illumination text printed on a high gloss paper (measuring approximately 86 per cent glare) was read as fast as on paper with less than 23 per cent glare (248). Tinker has concluded that with text printed in black ink all paper surfaces whether white or tinted with a reflectance of 70% or more are equally legible. In the normal reading situation, black print on a white ground is over 10 per cent more efficient than white on black (242, 316). Because brightness contrast is reduced, black ink on colour paper or colour inks on white are also less legible than black on white (119).

Looking for a:

S-c. fur. hol. flt. for 3 adlts., only 3 min. frm. sea by Astn. Mrtn.

Look in:

Dltns. Wkly.

There is an increasing use of 'abbreviated language', of contractions and other space saving devices, in many areas of printing. The classified advertisement columns of newspapers, provide many examples, and in Britain over 800 abbreviations of Christian names, addresses, and business descriptions are regularly used in telephone directories. Alternative abbreviations abound, however, and there is a need for rationalisation.

Harris & Cohen Ltd, 10 Green La, Thornton Hth...01-764 7104
Harris & Co, Est Agts, Survyrs,
    52 Golders Gn Rd NW11...01-455 1014
Harris & Co, Furrs, 2 Mill St W1...01-629 1942
Harris & Co. (Reigate) Ltd, Bldrs Mchts,
    15 West St...Reigate 43377
Harris & Co. (Veneers) Ltd, Mchts, Mfrs,
    103 Shoreditch High St E11...01-739 6199
    ...01-730 5541
Harris & Co, Whsle Tbcnsts, Confecs,
    106a West St...Erith 37155
Harris C. & T. (Calne) Ltd, Bacon Curers,
    Bilton Way, Enfield...01-804 5141
    48 Beddington La, Croydon...01-684 2095
    Do....01-684 9173
    Beresford Av, Wembley...01-903 4041
Harris David A.J, Solrs, 9 Parkway NW1...01-485 3383
Harris David & Son Ltd, Whsle Grcrs,
    Cherry Tree Rd...Watford 41371
Harris D. & Co.Ltd, Imptrs & Exptrs,
    1 Grangeway NW6...01-624 0857
Harris Defries (Textiles) Ltd, 5 Bywell Pl W1...01-580 6741
Harris D.F, Physn, 7 Princes St EC2...01-606 6159
Harris D.G, Est Agt, 167 Earls Ct Rd SW5...01-373 4921
Harris Displays Ltd, Exhibition Contrs,
    24 Charteris Rd NW6...01-328 2723
Harris & Dixon Ltd, Shipownrs, Ins Broks,
    81 Gracechurch St EC3...01-626 5631
    ...01-626 1996
Harris Dobby & Partners Ltd,
    Briset Ho, Briset St EC1...01-253 5157
Harris, Drprs, 40 Denmark Hl SE5...01-274 3750
Harris Dr.D.M. (Drs.Lorimer & Harris),
    23 Kings Av, Buckhurst Hl...01-504 0122
Harris D.R. & Co.Ltd, Dispng Chemst,
    29 St.James's St SW1...01-930 3915
    ...01-930 8753
Harris D.T. & Sons, Whsle Tbcnst, Confec,
    Wellington Ho, Messeter Pl SE9...01-850 2167
    ...01-850 9696
Harris Dudley, Photog, 44a Pentonville Rd N1...01-837 2533
Harris Dudley W. & Co.Ltd, Est Agts, Auctnrs,
    1 Station Rd...Sunbury-on-T 85288
    High St...Staines 55185
    Do....Staines 55422
    High St, Feltham...01-890 2607
    47 High St...Egham 3161
Harris E.C. & Partners, Chrtd Qty Survyrs,
    Manor Ho, London Rd, Mitcham...01-648 8186
    Lynton Ho, Tavistock Sq WC1...01-387 8431
    Tudor Chmbs, Station Rd, Pitsea...Vange 2727
    Do....Vange 3102
Harris & Edgar Ltd, Masonry Fixings,
    21 Progress Wy, Croydon...01-686 4891
    222 Purley Wy, Croydon...01-686 4891
Harris Dr.Edw, Schwartz Dr.Morris,
    135 High Rd, Chadwell Hth...01-590 1461
Harris Electrical Ltd,...01-985 1637
    101 Lower Clapton Rd E5...01-985 6388
Harris E. (Builder) Ltd,...01-866 5843
    (Off & Yd) 87 Paines La, Pinner...01-866 7989
Harris E. & L. (London) Ltd, Mntl Mfrs,
    6 Palatine Rd N16...01-254 5461
Harris Engineering Co.Ltd,
    York Wks, Browning St SE17...01-703 7841
Harris E. & Son (Coventry) Ltd, Bldrs,
    57 Uxbridge Rd W5...01-567 6275
Harris Estates, Est Agts, Val, Station App...Billericay 3183
Harris F. (Carpet Planners) Ltd,
    73 Curtain Rd EC2...01-739 6166
Harris F. & G.Ltd, Bldrs & Contrs,
    136 Lambeth Rd SE1...01-928 2269
Harris Frank (Blouses) Ltd, Mfrs,
    83 Mortimer St W1...01-580 1328
Harris Frederic R. & Partners, Conslt Engs,
    10 Storeys Gte SW1...01-839 2461
Harris F. & Sons (Butchers) Ltd,...01-435 2413
    17 Heath St NW3...01-435 3446
Harris F. (Stonemasons) Ltd, British Rly Gds
    Depot, Sterne St W12...01-743 8861
    Goods Yd...01-743 5056
Harris Funnell & Co. Chrtd Acctnts,
    19 Harewood Rd, S Croydon...01-688 2224
Harris F.W. & Sons Ltd, Outftrs & Furns,
    172 Goldhawk Rd W12...01-743 2314
Harris G.C.Ltd, Archtl Metal Wks,...01-730 3248
    172 Buckingham Pal Rd SW1...01-730 7035
Harris G.C.W. (Tadworth) Ltd, Bldg Contrs,...Tadworth 2333
    Chequers La, Walton-on-the-Hill...Tadworth 2475
Harris Geoffrey (Bibby Off), 5a Castle St...Tonbridge 4494
Harris George & Bros. (Frames) Ltd,...01-387 1368
    37 Camden High St NW1...01-387 1923
Harris G.H, Bakeries Ltd,...01-639 3928
    905 Old Kent Rd SE15...01-639 5582
Harris & Gillow, Survyrs, Auctnrs, Est Agts,
    93 Wardour St W1...01-437 2504
Harris & Goldring Ltd, Whsle,
    1a Wendover Rd NW10...01-965 6673
Harris Gordon & Barton, Chrtd Qty Survyrs,
    7 Connaught Pl W2...01-723 9281
Harris & Graham Ltd, Ins Broks,
    52 Lime St EC3...01-626 9681
Harris & Graham Pattinson & Co, Life Pension
    Conslts, 23 Chandos Ct, Caxton St SW1...01-799 1571
Harris & Graham Pattinson Robson Ltd,
    52 Lime St EC3...01-626 5905
Harris & Graham (Shipping) Ltd,
    52 Lime St EC3...01-626 0487
Harris H, Jwlrs, 12 Piccadilly Arc SW1...01-629 7996
Harris H. (Jewellers) Ltd, 44 Hatton Gdn EC1...01-405 6265
    175 Deptford High St SE8...01-692 1386
Harris H, Turf Acctnt, 38 Coram St WC1...01-837 8656
Harris Harold A, Solr, Albany Court Yd W1...01-734 2211
Harris Harold & Co, Solrs, 31 Church La, E11...01-539 8275
Harris Haulage (Grays) Ltd, Contrs...Purfleet 5340
    Forge Gar, London Rd, W Thurrock...Purfleet 6413
Harris H. & Co. (Reclamation) Ltd, Txtl Wastes,
    1a Oldershaw Rd N7...01-607 1685
Harris Henry H, Barrstr, 3 Hare Ct, Temple EC4...01-353 3344
Harris H.I, Ophthal Optcns,...01-902 0271
    12 Park La, Wembley...01-902 1878

Harris Howard & Co, Est Agts,
    62 Crouch End Hl N8...01-340 7645
Harris Howell J, Catrer, 51 Petty France SW1...01-222 7587
Harris H. & Sons (Furniture) Ltd,
    1 Grimsby St E2...01-739 5655
Harris H.T, Btchr, 41 Great Titchfield St W1...01-636 4228
Harris H. (Textiles) Ltd, Furns Fabrics,
    58 Great Eastern St EC2...01-739 8921
Harris & Hunter Ltd, Pblc Relations,...01-836 0144
    69 New Oxford St WC1...01-836 2184
Harris Interior Contracts Ltd,
    24 Charteris Rd NW6...01-328 2723
Harris J, 135 High St, Barkingside...01-550 8762
Harris Jack (Footwear) Ltd,...01-580 2922
    296 Regent St W1...01-580 5772
Harris Jack & Son Ltd, Commn Agt,
    2 Station Pde, Ickenham Rd...Ruislip 36614
Harris Dr.J.Armstrong, Psychiatrist,
    138 Harley St W1...01-935 6570
Harris J.C. & Associates, Conslt Structl Engs,
    53 Kilburn High Rd NW6...01-624 8146
Harris J. (Diamonds) Ltd, 44 Hatton Gdn EC1...01-405 6265
Harris (Jewellery) Ltd, 1 Market Wy E14...01-987 1500
    Do....01-987 3548
    264 Heathway, Dagenham...01-592 5681
    (Head Off) 8 South St...Romford 45151
Harris John (Bermondsey) Ltd, Hlge,...01-698 7291
    141 Sangley Rd, SE6...01-698 8223
Harris John (Cartage) Ltd, Road Hlge Contrs,
    Denmark Ho, Tooley St SE1...01-407 7561
Harris John (Plant Hire) Ltd,
    141 Sangley Rd SE6...01-698 7291
Harris John R, FRIBA, 24 Devonshire Pl W1...01-935 0861
Harris John & Son (London) Ltd, Spir Varnish
    Mfrs, Cox La, Chessington...01-397 2161
Harris John (Tools) Ltd, Mfrs,
    86 Greenfield Rd E1...01-247 0695
Harris Johnson & Co, Crpt Planners,
    272b Chatham Av, Nile St N1...01-253 6369
Harris J.P, Barrstr,
    12 Kings Bench Wlk, Temple EC4...01-353 7008
Harris J. & R.Ltd, Clothg Mfrs, Bush Fair...Harlow 21123
Harris J.Seymour & Partners, Archts,
    Carrara Ho, Embankment Pl WC2...01-930 5221
Harris Kafton & Co, Chrtd Acctnts,...01-493 4364
    23 Albemarle St W1...01-499 3384
Harris Lebus Ltd, Furn Mfrs, (Share Transfer
    Off) Lee Ho, London Wall EC2...01-606 7051
    (Showrooms) 17 Maddox St W1...01-493 9871
Harris Leigh Fabrics Ltd,...Watford 20783
    1 Faircross Ho, High St...Watford 29780
Harris Leonard Ltd, House Furnishers,
    8 Woodhouse Rd N12...01-445 2277
Harris Lew (Extra) Ltd, Turf Acctnts,
    118 Newgate St EC1...01-606 5421
    131 Whitecross St EC1...01-253 2572
Harris Lew (London) Ltd, Turf Acctnts,
    58 Cannon St EC4...01-248 6782
Harris Lewis S, Assr, 35 Riverside Dv NW11...01-455 4206
Harris L. (Harella) Ltd, Ladies Coats, Suits,
    Skirts, (Shwrm) 87 New Bond St W1...01-629 5017
    Do....01-629 6547
    (Facty) 90 Goswell Rd EC1...01-253 8871
Harris Lifting & Shipping Tackle Ltd,
    35 New Broad St EC2...01-588 2977
Harris L.M. & Co, Chrtd Acctnts,
    68 Coleman St EC2...01-638 0977
Harris L. (Menswear) Ltd, Tlr,
    221a Whitechapel Rd E1...01-247 8894
    1 Fulbourne St E1...01-247 8894
Harris L.S. & Co. (Assessors) Ltd, Survyrs, Vals,...01-262 4571
    83 Crawford St W1...01-262 5561
    366 City Rd EC1...01-837 6151
    Do....01-837 6372
Harris L.Taylor, Solr, 6 Surrey St WC2...01-836 7241
Harris & Marsh Ltd, Road Transp Contrs,
    Station Chmbs, Woodcote Rd, Wallington...FRAnklin 2181
Harris Michael, Barrstr, 2 Garden Ct EC4...01-353 4741
Harris M.M, Ins Brok, 359 Romford Rd E7...01-534 6345
Harris M.P. & Co.Ltd, Bldrs Mchts,
    Kingston Rd...Leatherhead 3496
Harris M. & Sons, Antiq Furn, Wks of Art,
    44 New Oxford St WC1...01-636 2121
Harris Muriel Ltd, 9 Harley St W1...01-636 3833
Harris N. & Co, Acctnts,
    157a Clapham High St SW4...01-622 0181
Harris Overseas Ltd, Import & Export,
    120 Ripple Rd, Barking...01-594 1473
Harris Paul Associates, 58 Harleyford Rd SE11...01-735 9681
Harris Pencils Co.The,...01-953 2108
    Imperial Stus, Elstree Wy, Boreham Wd...01-953 2118
Harris P.B, Solr, 8 Church La...E Grinstead 23687
    Imperial Stus, Elstree Wy, Boreham Wd...01-953 2118
Harris Peter B.Ltd, Tbcnsts,...01-935 3275
    75 Marylebone High St W1...01-935 6122
    4 Barnes High St SW13...01-876 4994
    11 Strutton Ground SW1...01-799 2772
Harris Peter G, Inc Survyr & Est Agt,...01-499 1780
    9 Down St W1...01-499 5026
Harris & Philip-Ltd, Commn Agts,
    22 Featherstone Rd, Southall...01-574 2399
Harris & Philp (Shops) Ltd, Turf Acctnts,...01-574 1280
    22 Featherstone Rd, Southall...01-574 4140
Harris & Philp (Staines) Ltd, Turf Acctnts,
    2 Norris Rd...Staines 54182
Harris P.J.B,
    Station Chmbs, Woodcote Rd, Wallington...01-669 1866
Harris P.J. & Partner Ltd, Property Dlrs,
    357 Upper Richmond Rd Wst SW14...01-876 0111
Harris Plating Works Ltd.The, Electro-Platers,
    18 New Wharf Rd N1...01-837 7263
Harris & Porter, Chrtd Qty Survyr,
    Watergate Ho, York Bldgs WC2...01-839 6064
Harris P.T, Chemst, 187 Kings Rd SW3...01-352 1785
    Do....01-352 5756
Harris P.T. (1960) Ltd, Chemsts,...01-584 3415
    10 Palace Gte W8...01-584 3832
Harris Publications Ltd, Philatelic,
    27 Maiden La WC2...01-240 1006
Harris Raymond & Dollar, Acctnts,...01-242 4554
    5 Staple Inn WC1...01-242 7521

The earliest age at which a woman can draw a retirement pension is 60. On her own insurance she can get a pension when she reaches that age, if she has then retired from regular employment. Otherwise she has to wait until she retires or reaches age 65. At age 65 pension can be paid irrespective of retirement. On her husband's insurance, however, she cannot get a pension, even though she is over 60, until he has reached age 65 and retired from regular employment, or until he is 70 if he does not retire before reaching that age.

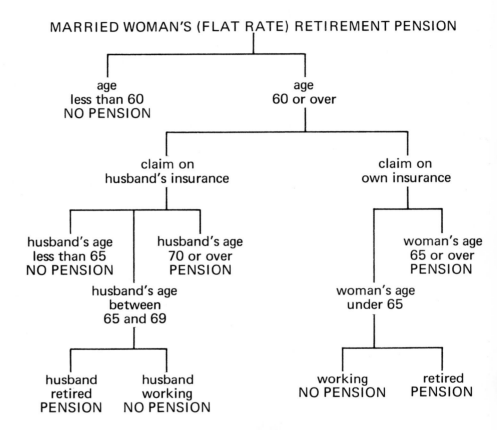

MARRIED WOMAN'S (FLAT RATE) RETIREMENT PENSION

1	I am under 60	Yes: No:	NO PENSION read Question 2
2	I am claiming	(a) on my own insurance (b) on my husband's insurance	read Question 3 read Question 5
3	I am under 65	Yes: No:	read Question 4 PENSION
4	I am working	Yes: No:	NO PENSION PENSION
5	my husband's age is	(a) less than 65 (b) between 65 and 69 (c) 70 or more	NO PENSION read Question 6 PENSION
6	my husband has retired	Yes: No:	PENSION NO PENSION

Summary

Words set entirely in capitals are considerably less legible than words in lower case. Italics reduce legibility but, provided the counters of the letters are open, bold face does not. Semi-bold types are preferred by many readers. For people with poor vision, semi-bold type is essential.

Excessively long lines cause a sharp increase in the number of regressions. Short lines, on the other hand, increase the number of fixation pauses.

Leading permits line length to be extended without loss of legibility.

There is no appreciable loss of legibility when type is printed in black ink on tinted paper provided this is of 70% reflectance or more.

Black print on white is more legible than white on black.

Legibility is not significantly affected by the use of paper of high or low gloss, but well diffused illumination is important.

Unjustified setting does not decrease legibility.

Reading efficiency is severely reduced by any departure from the horizontal, and by departure from the 90° angle in reading.

A number of non-optimum factors combined, though not strictly cumulative, may drastically reduce reading efficiency.

Towards a new alphabet

The roman alphabet is used in more than 60 countries and by over 600 million people. Over 300 million people speak the English language. Some languages are alphabetically efficient - by which is meant that their alphabets represent the sounds of the languages exactly - or nearly so. But English is very non-alphabetic and English spelling is an unreliable guide to pronunciation.

During the past century, many proposals have been put forward for revising our alphabet. Some of these proposals, such as those for type faces of novel design published by Javal (142) in 1881, by Millington (218) in 1883, and Cohn and Rübencamp (65) in 1903, have been inspired by the search for improved legibility. Other proposals have been advanced with the aim of establishing a greater correspondence between written and spoken language. Some designers, recognising that the printed rather than the inscriptional or handwritten letter has become the norm, have attempted to rationalise and simplify the design of our existing alphabet by constructing the letters from geometrical components; others have suggested entirely new sets of signs. Some writers have argued in favour of a single alphabet composed entirely of lower case, others have proposed the use of capitals only or a single alphabet made up of a combination of capital and lower case letters. There have been proposals for reducing the number of signs we employ as well as for increasing the range of signs to correspond with the number of basic sounds in English. And in recent years developments in electronics have inspired a host of new designs for 'alpha-numeric characters'.

Among the most interesting of these proposals are those of Bayer, Piggott, and Read. All advocate a single alphabet, and Bayer and Piggott favour a modified version of the existing lower case alphabet - greatly extended in the case of Bayer, and contracted (by the omission of Q) in the case of Piggott. Herbert Bayer's 'fonetik alfabet' attempts to relate each sign to a single sound. Double letters, such as ch, sh, and th, are replaced with new single characters and Bayer has introduced single signs for word endings and syllables such as ed, en, ion, ing, ng, ory. Bayer's design is essentially monoline, geometrical, sanserif, but Piggott has demonstrated that his proposal is effective both as a serif face and as a sanserif, and also in a variety of weights and widths (263). An especially important feature of Piggott's design is that all letters are of common width. Kingsley Read's phonetic alphabet, designed in response to the demands of George Bernard Shaw's Will, is a considerably more drastic innovation. It consists of over forty signs. Four frequently recurring words are each represented by a single sign, and proper names are indicated by a dot.

New media and new techniques of reproducing the visible word are providing new opportunities for alphabetic communication as well as imposing changes in the design of the signs we employ. The reconsideration of our alphabet is, therefore, no longer merely a theoretical exercise but an activity which, on practical grounds, it is today both desirable and opportune to pursue with vigour. But however desirable technically, aesthetically or phonetically the introduction of a wholly new set of signs might seem - and despite the fact that we can learn to read even an entirely new alphabet, such as Kingsley Read's, very much more quickly than most of us imagine - the practical and economic disadvantages of such a change create a formidable barrier to any movement in that direction. A more rewarding direction for alphabet reform is likely to be towards a single alphabet composed of many of our present signs (but with those which are redundant eliminated, and those which are confusing replaced with less ambiguous signs) augmented with a sufficient number of additional signs to permit our alphabet to be used phonetically (without requiring that it must be so used). The basic design of the signs must be considered and developed in relation to the requirements of all visual media, and be such as will allow a variety of design interpretations. A single standard typeface, though it has much to commend it on functional grounds for many kinds of alphabetic communication, can never be adequate for all purposes since typographic allusion or 'congeniality', in which the shape and visual weight of letters plays an important role, is a vital though temporaly unstable factor in many kinds of printing and graphic design.

Half-uncial typewriter face proposed by Kaufmann in 1911.

AUS GROSSBUCHSTABEN BESTEH
ENDE NEUE SCHRIFT MIT
STARK BEMERKBAREN UBERHÖH-
UNGEN,ÄHNLICH UNSERER ALTGE-
WOHNTEN KERNSCHRIFT. SIE
BESITZT GENAU DIESEL-
BEN EINPRÄGSAMEN WORTBILDER

fur den noien menſen eksistirt nur das glaihgeviht tsviſen natur unt gaist· tsu jedem tsaitpuʌkt der fergaʌenhait varen ale variatsjonen des alten ›noi‹· aber es var niht ›das‹ noie· vir dürfen niht fergesen· das vir an ainer vende der kultur ſtehen· am ende ales alten·

MŪSJK JM Lēben dēr VÖLKER AM 2.JŪLJ 20 Ūhr dJRJGJert JM OPERNhAUS WARShAUS berŪhmter dJRJGENT WERKE POLNJ5her MEJSter PREJSe 1–5Mk.

Hier handelt es sich nicht mehr um eine lediglich dekorative Umwandlung abgegriffener Themen, sondern ganz im Gegenteil um die Schöpfung eines neuen Themas, dem die Fähigkeit innewohnt, von kommenden Moden und Stilen abgewandelt zu werden und neuen künstlerischen Bemühungen als Ausgangspunkt zu dienen. Eindringendes Studium der geschichtlichen Entwicklung der Schriftformen brachte uns die Gewissheit, dass diese Entwicklung grundsätzlich sinngemäss fortgeführt

abcdefghi jklmnopqr stuvwxyz a d d

The phonetic alphabet designed by Kingsley. Read in response to the demands of Shaw's Will consists of over forty letters. It is a single alphabet and proper names are indicated by a preceding 'namer' dot. The four most frequent words (the, of, and, to) are each represented by a single letter. The illustration opposite shows its greater economy of space.

	Short	Short	
if	I	५	eat
egg	८	८	age
ash	↗	↗	ice
ado	↗	↗	up
on	↘	○	oak
wool	V	Λ	ooze
out	↙	↗	oil
ah	↗	↗	awe
are	↗	↗	or
air	↗	↗	err
array	↗	↗	ear

	Tall		
Ian	↗	↗	yew

	Tall	Deep	
peep	↗	↗	bib
tot	↗	↗	dead
kick	↗	↗	gag
fee	↗	↗	vow
thigh	↗	↗	they
so	↗	↗	zoo
sure	↗	↗	meaSure
church	↗	↗	judge
yea	↗	↗	woe
hung	↗	↗	ha-ha

	Short	Short	
loll	↗	↗	roar
mime	↗	↗	nun

Speech-tracing symbols for the sounds of English: vowels with downstrokes.

bit	bet	bat	but	box	bull
		bar	bird	bought	
bead	bait			boat	boot
bite	bough			boy	few
	ballot				

Speech-tracing symbols for the sounds of English: consonants with upstrokes or sideways.

pip	bib	fluff	valve	mum	
tit	did	thigh	thy	nun	
kick	gag	loch (Scots)	sing		
cease	zoos	shoe	vision	church	judge
hay	you	way	why	rural	lull

60

LAVINIA [*composedly*] Yes, Captain: they love even their enemies.

THE CAPTAIN. Is that easy?

LAVINIA. Very easy, Captain, when their enemies are as handsome as you.

THE CAPTAIN. Lavinia: you are laughing at me.

LAVINIA. At you, Captain! Impossible.

THE CAPTAIN. Then you are flirting with me, which is worse. Dont be foolish.

LAVINIA. But such a very handsome captain.

THE CAPTAIN. Incorrigible! [*Urgently*] Listen to me. The men in that audience tomorrow will be the vilest of voluptuaries: men in whom the only passion excited by a beautiful woman is a lust to see her tortured and torn shrieking limb from limb. It is a crime to gratify that passion. It is offering yourself for violation by the whole rabble of the streets and the riff-raff of the court at the same time. Why will you not choose rather a kindly love and an honorable alliance?

LAVINIA. They cannot violate my soul. I alone can do that by sacrificing to false gods.

THE CAPTAIN. Sacrifice then to the true God. What does his name matter? We call him Jupiter. The Greeks call him Zeus. Call him what you will as you drop the incense on the altar flame; He will understand.

LAVINIA. No. I couldnt. That is the strange thing, Captain, that a little pinch of incense should

The system called Speech-tracing was developed by Felix von Kunowski about thirty years ago and is now in use by children in some sixty schools in Western Germany. The symbols have here been related to the sounds of English by Christopher Matthews.

This alphabet for Speech-tracing has been proved suitable by

its practical use in correspondence between many people, and by

the ease with which children have learnt it and used it for a quick

transition to the conventional script.

ho𝗐 much is expendable

abcdefghijklmnopqrstuvwxyz

an alphabet designed as part of an experiment
to determine how much of each letter of the
lower case alphabet could be eliminated without
seriously affecting legibility

An alphabet, above, designed by Brian Coe
as part of an experiment to determine how
much of each letter of the lower case
alphabet could be eliminated without
seriously affecting legibility.

Opposite: a proposal for a new alphabet by
Reginald Piggott. He calls it National Roman
and he has eliminated the letter Q which he
regards as unnecessary in the English
language. An important feature of this
design is that all letters are of common
width. The illustration at the foot shows a
comparison of the relative face and body
sizes of National Roman and Bembo.

speaking of bird life in palestine, it might interest and
surprise many people to know

speaking of bird life in palestine,
it might interest and surprise many
people to know that in this appar-

speaking of bird life in palestine, it might interest and
surprise many people to know that in this apparently bird
less land, there are over four hundred species. all these

abcdefghjklmnopr

abcdefghjklmnopr

E13B, developed by American Bankers
Association in 1958.

0 1 2 3 4 5 6 7 8 9 ⑈⬛

CMC7, sponsored by European Computer
Manufacturers Association, Geneva.

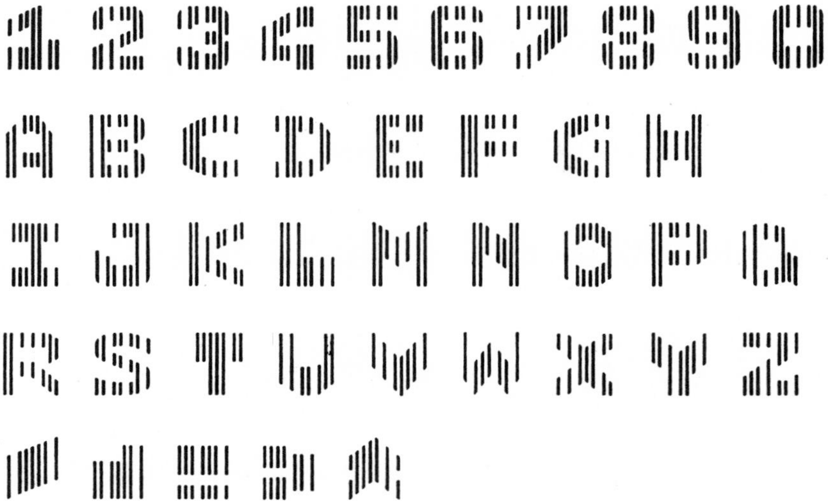

1 2 3 4 5 6 7 8 9 0

A B C D E F G H

I J K L M N O P

R S T U V W X Y Z

OCR-A

1 2 3 4 5 6 7 8 9 0

♫ ϒ H I

A B C D E F G H I J K L M N O P

Q R S T U V W X Y Z

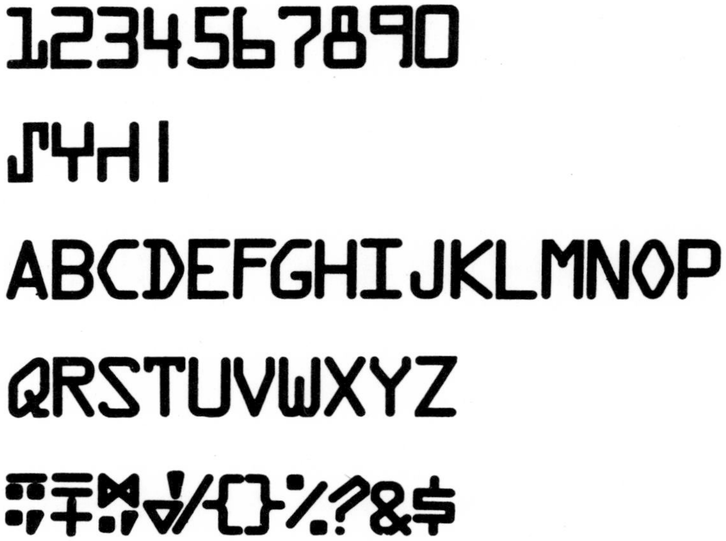

OCR-B

ABCDEFGH abcdefgh
IJKLMNOP ijklmnop
QRSTUVWX qrstuvwx
YZ*+,-./ yz m åøæ
01234567 £$:;<%>?
89   [@!#&,]
          (=) "´`^ ~ ˇ
ÄÖÅÑÜÆØ   ↑≤≥×÷°¤

The characters shown opposite were
developed by engineers to satisfy the
requirements of electronic reading methods.
E13B and CMC7 are for use with magnetic
inks, while OCR-A is for use with optical
character reading equipment. OCR-B, shown
above, was developed by the European
Computer Manufacturers Association with
the aim of producing a font which would
both satisfy the requirements of OCR
systems and be acceptable as a general
purpose type. The result is the product of
collaboration between engineers and a
designer, Adrian Frutiger.

65

A typeface for machine recognition,
developed by Epps and Evans at the
National Physical Laboratory (Division of
Computer Science), which avoids curves and
diagonals.

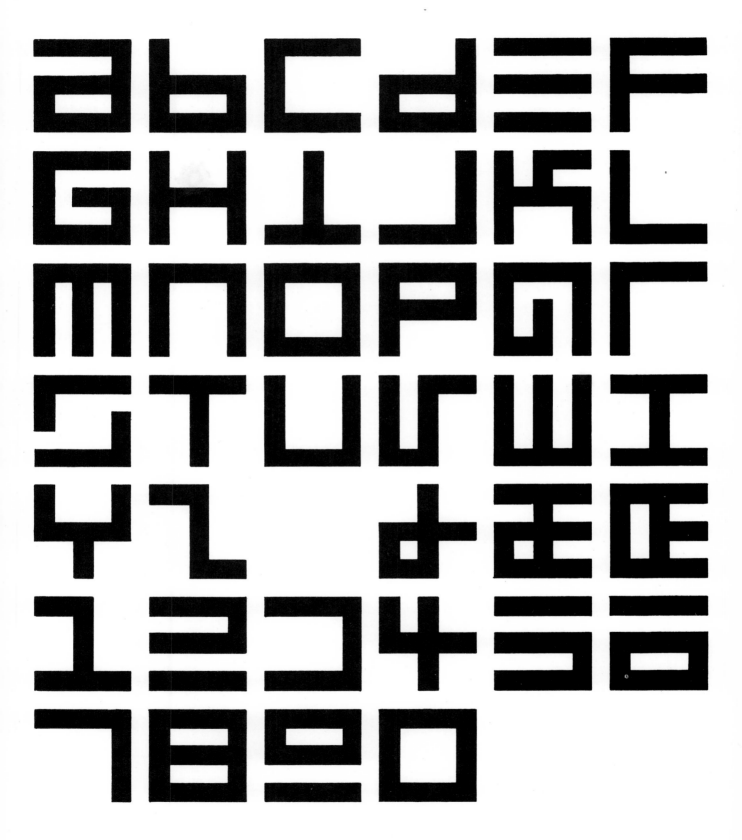

Wim Crouwel's design for an alphabet designed particularly to satisfy the requirements of cathode ray tube typesetting is shown opposite. All characters are of common width. The illustration on this page, in which an enlarged 'scanned' letter 'a' in Garamond and in Crouwel's alphabet are compared, demonstrates the superiority for this purpose of Crouwel's design over conventional letter forms.

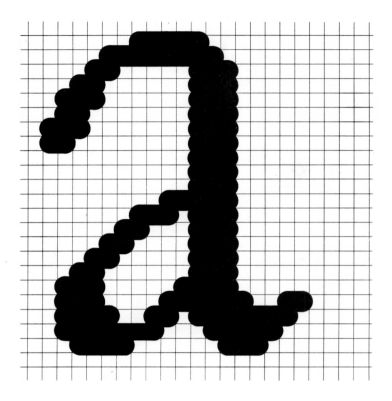

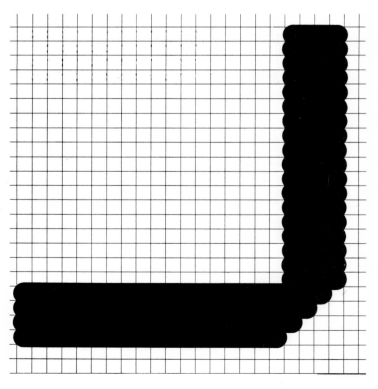

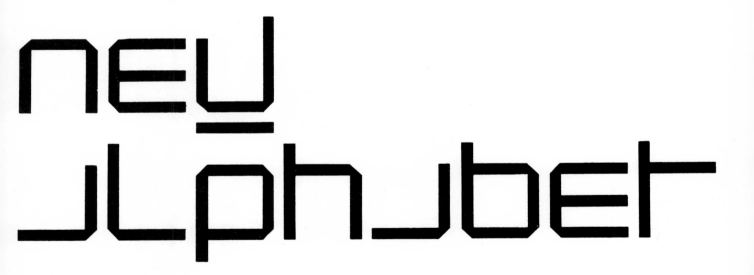

A type face, known as CBS News 36, developed by the Graphic Arts Department of CBS News to withstand the particular distortions of television broadcasting.

ABCDEFG
HIJKLMN
OPQRSTU
VWXYZ

abcdefgh
ijklmnopq
rstuvwxyz
12345678
90$¢&%
(/-'""?.,:;!)

A comparison of News Gothic Bold (a,b)
with the specially designed CBS News (c,d)
In the latter enlargements there is less light
flux and spread, the counters are more open,
and the inside corners less rounded.

2

1   3   4

Increasingly, messages are converted from one medium to another over which the originator may have no control. These illustrations of part of a magazine page, reproduced actual size, show how the image may be degraded in the copying process.

1 Printed by offset-litho.
2 Microfiche made from 1.
3 Electrostatic copy of 1.
4,5,6 Prints made from microfiche 2 in a typical monobath reader printer with variations in the exposure time.
7 Xerox copy of 6 made to provide a more permanent record.

With acknowledgements to the National Reprographic Centre for Documentation, Hatfield College of Technology.

american maiz
continued from page 21

Next, a production pl copy is made from the ter and the master rou the production plannir where other variable ir such as routing, wareho ences, etc. is added. Th then checked for accuracy ies are run off for the sh tion, control lab, sales o diter, and loading crews. ors are used for the first green for the loading tall uling supervisors indicate able date for shipment c copies of the order.

The file copy is retain duction planning, a copy the control lab for inforn poses. The other copies sales order expediter. shipping date is added ar ies released to the shipp and loading crew invo

For **AC**
INFORI

american maiz
continued from page 21

Next, a production p copy is made from the ter and the master rou the production planni where other variable j such as routing, wareh ences, etc. is added. T then checked for accurac ies are run off for the sh tion, control lab, sales c diter, and loading crews ors are used for the firs green for the loading tal uling supervisors indicat able date for shipment copies of the order.

The file copy is retair duction planning, a cop the control lab for infori poses. The other copies sales order expediter. shipping date is added a ies released to the shipp and loading crew inv

For **AC**
INFOR

american ma
continued from page 21

Next, a production copy is made from th ter and the master i the production plan where other variable such as routing, war ences, etc. is added. then checked for accur ies are run off for the tion, control lab, sales diter, and loading crev ors are used for the fi green for the loading t uling supervisors indic able date for shipment copies of the order.

The file copy is reta duction planning, a co the control lab for info poses. The other copi sales order expediter. shipping date is added ies released to the ship and loading crew in

For **AC**
INFOR

6   7

american maize
nued from page 21

ext, a production plar
is made from the or
and the master .route
production planning
e other variable inf
as routing, warehou
s, etc. is added. The
checked for accuracy,
re run off for the ship
control lab, sales ord
, and loading crews.
are used for the first t
n for the loading tailie
supervisors indicate
date for shipment on
s of the order.
he file copy is retained
ion planning, a copy i
control lab for informa
s. The other copies g
order expediter. H
ping date is added and
cleased to the shippin
loading crew invol

american maize
continued from page 21

Next, a production plar
copy is made from the or
ter and the master route
the production planning
where other variable inf
such as routing, warehou
ences, etc. is added. The
then checked for accuracy,
ies are run off for the ship
tion, control lab, sales ord
diter, and loading crews.
ors are used for the first t
green for the loading tailie
uling supervisors indicate
able date for shipment on
copies of the order.
The file copy is retained
duction planning, a copy i
the control lab for informa
poses. The other copies g
sales order expediter. H
shipping date is added and
ies released to the shippin
and loading crew invol

american maize
continued from page 21

Next, a production planning file
copy is made from the order master and the master routed within
the production planning section
where other variable information,
such as routing, warehouse refer-
ences, etc. is added. The order is
then checked for accuracy, and copies are run off for the shipping section, control lab, sales order expediter, and loading crews. Pink col-
ors are used for the first three and
green for the loading tallies. Sched-
uling supervisors indicate an available date for shipment on all pink
copies of the order.

The file copy is retained by production planning, a copy is sent to
the control lab for information purposes. The other copies go to the
sales order expediter. Here, the
shipping date is added and the copies released to the shipping section
and loading crew involved. The

loading crew gets three copies in
the case of rail shipments and two
for trucks, each copy bearing a
rectangular diagram on the bottom
to show loading rotation.

Next, a tentative shipping date is
wired to New York, and the day
prior to the actual shipment an "expect to ship" wire is sent. The objective is to ship on the originally
listed available date, but loading
priorities, special equipment needs,
and other factors may alter the
plan. When a shipment actually
goes out a confirmation of the shipment is sent.

Each order master is filed in the
shipping section. Then, when the
loading tallies come back to signi-
fy a shipment is ready, the senior
shipping clerk compares the master and the loading tally, assigns
the shipper's number and makes
any changes that might be necessary on the master. Pohndorff said
that any number of variables, such
as differing weights or quantities

ʌn ʌlfʌbɛt ko-ɔrdinætɪ̩ fonɛtiks ʌnd visɪ̩n wil̪ bɛ æ mǫr ɛf̪ɛktiv tul uf kumunikætɪ̩n

ʌ b c d ε f ɕ ɦ i j k l m n

a ƃ   d ε   ɡ   k

ε   ɢ

e

o p q ʀ s t u v w x y z

ʀ   т

ʀ

ᴦ ᴦ ᴦ ᴦ

Herbert Bayer's 'fonetik alfabet' in which the individual letter forms have been simplified and each sign relates to a single sound. The use of double letters, such as ch, th, sh, is eliminated by the introduction of new single characters and new symbols have been added for sound groups, word endings and syllables, such as ed, en, ion, ing, ng, ory. Letters not pronounced are omitted.

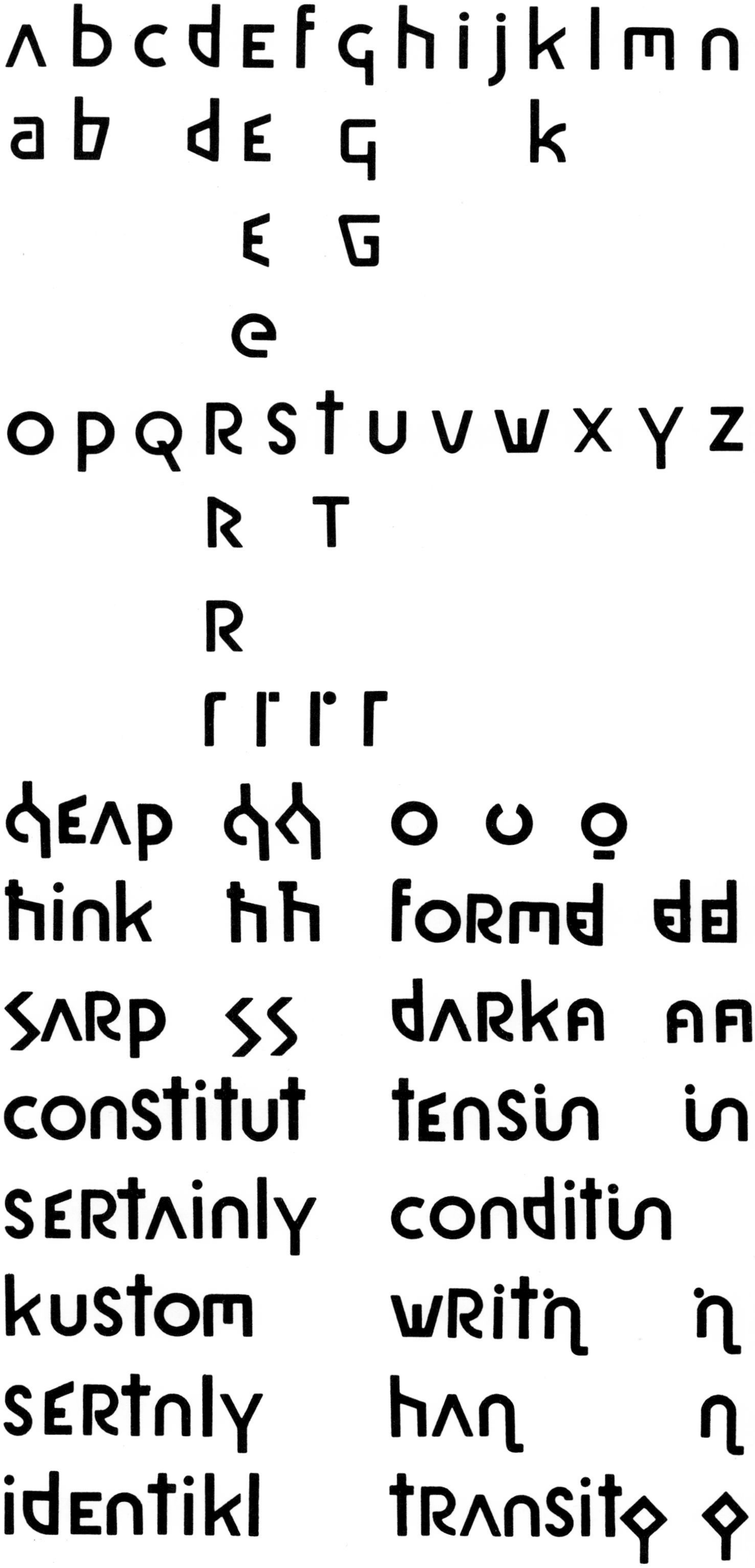

SERᴦ

ɕεʌp ɕɕ   o ʋ ǫ

ɦink ɦɦ   foʀmd ƌƌ

sʌʀp ss   dʌʀkʌ ʌꟼ

constitut   tεnsiɳ   iɳ

sεʀtʌinly   conditiɳ

kustom   wʀitɳ   �215n

sεʀtɳly   ɦʌn   ɳ

idεntikl   tʀʌnsitǫ ǫ

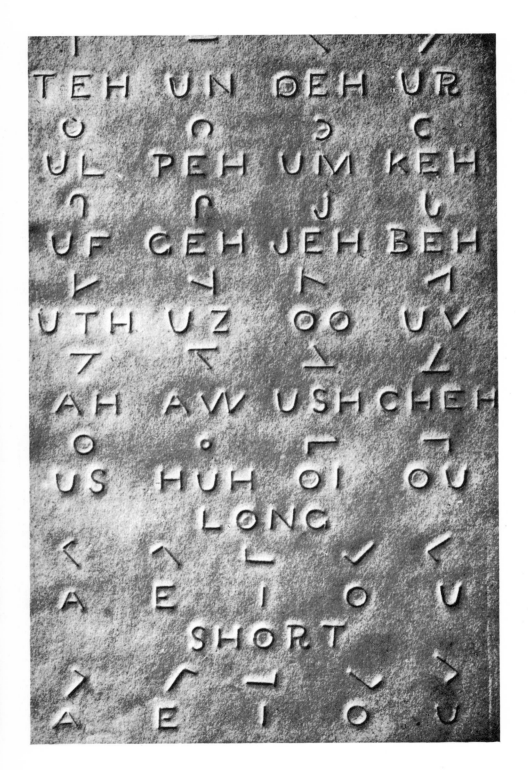

The blind 'read' by touch and the Braille system is used internationally. But there is another method, shown opposite, which was invented by Dr William Moon in 1847. 'Moon' is often preferred by those who lose their sight later in life, and it is of interest because many characters relate closely to the normal alphabet but only the essential strokes are retained. Some of Moon's letters were based on the earlier, phonetic system devised by Frere (left).

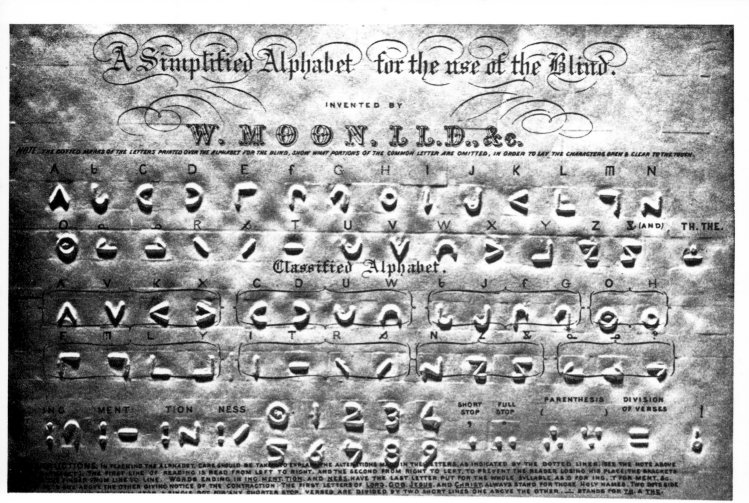

A Simplified Alphabet for the use of the Blind.

INVENTED BY

W. MOON, LL.D., &c.

wuns upon a tiem littl red hen livd in a barn with her fiev chicks. a pig, a cat and a duck mæd thær hœm in the sæm barn. ɛɛch dæ littl red hen led her chicks out tœ lœk for fœd. but the pig, the cat and the duck wœd not lœk for fœd.

æ face	b bed	c cat	d dog	ɛɛ key
f feet	g leg	h hat	ie fly	j jug	k key
l letter	m man	n nest	œ over	p pen	ɼ girl
r red	s spoon	t tree	ue use	v voice	w window
y yes	z zebra	ƺ daisy	wh when	ch chair
th three	th the	ʃh shop	ʒ television	ŋ ring
a father	au ball	a cap	e egg	i milk	o box
u up	ω book	ꞷ spoon	ou out	oi oil

tiepografical deʃieners

wuns upon a tiem littl red hen livd
in a bahrn wiht her fiev chiks. a pig,
a cat and a duk maed thaer hoem in
the saem bahrn. eech dae littl red hen
led her chiks out too look for foood.
but the pig, the cat and the duk
wood not look for foood.

ae	b	c	d	ee
face	bed	cat	dog	see

f	g	h	ie	j	k
feet	go	hat	pie	jug	key

l	m	n	oe	p
letter	man	nest	over	pen

r	s	t	ue	v
red	soon	tie	use	voice

w	y	z	wh	ch
win	yes	zebra	when	chair

th	ht	sh	zh	ng
the	three	shop	television	sing

ah	au	a	e	i	o
father	ball	cap	egg	sick	box

u	oo	ooo	ou	oi
up	book	soon	out	oil

Pitman's Initial Teaching Alphabet, opposite,
is now used for teaching young children in
many schools.

Edward Rondthaler has proposed adapting
the principles of Pitman's augmented alphabet
to permit the use of normal lower case type,
as demonstrated above. In Rondthaler's
proposal for a 24-letter simplified phonetic
roman alphabet (published in Print magazine,
XVIII:1, 1964) 'x' is replaced by 'ks', and
'q' by 'kw'. Capitals are eliminated.

	OCR-B	Epps-Evans	OCR-A	CMC7	Piggott	Crouwel	Coe	Bayer		Moon	Bayer fonetik

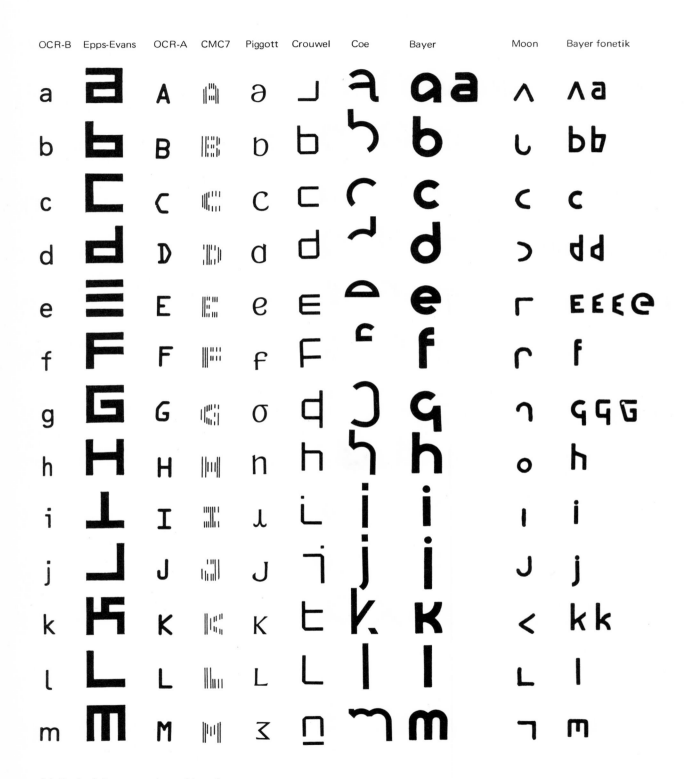

A letter by letter comparison of ten of
the alphabets shown on the preceding pages.

OCR-B	Epps-Evans	OCR-A	CMC7	Piggott	Crouwel	Coe	Bayer	Moon	Bayer fonetik
n									
o									
p									
q									
r									
s									
t									
u									
v									
w									
x									
y									
z									

Glossary

Ascender	The part of a lower case letter which rises above the mean-line, or level of the x-height, as in b, d, f, h, k, l
Black letter	A term for Old English, Gothic or Fraktur text
Coated paper	A paper surfaced with a smooth china-clay composition suitable for the high quality reproduction of photographs
Condensed	A narrow type design
Counter	The 'inner shape' or enclosed parts of a letter as in b, d, o, p, q, etc
Descender	The part of a lower case letter which projects below the base line as in g, j, p, q, y
Face	The printing surface of metal type. The word is also used to describe the design of type
Fount or font	Complete set of a particular size and design of type comprising lower case, capital and small capital alphabets, figures, punctuation marks, etc
Full point	A printer's term for a full stop
Indent	To begin a line with a blank space, setting the line back a little
Leading	Interlinear space. In metal-type composition thin strips of lead, below type height, are used to space out lines of type
Lower case	The small letters of a fount (a, b, c, etc) as opposed to the capitals and small capitals
Modern	A general term for type designs which have a strong vertical emphasis and straight hair line serifs
Pica	A printer's measurement approximately 1/6 of an inch (12 points)
Point	The standard of typographical measurement used by printers in England and America to indicate the body size of types. 72 points measure 0.9962", approximately 1"
Sanserif	A style of type which has no serifs
Serif	The finishing strokes at the top and bottom of a letter
Set	The amount of lateral spacing between letters. In metal-type composition this depends on the thickness of body apportioned to each character, and types are described as having 'wide' or 'narrow' set
Solid	Type set without any interlinear spacing, or 'leading'
Uncial	Rounded capital letters from which are derived lower case letters such as e, u, etc. A half uncial contains characteristics of both capital and lower case letters
x-height	The height of lower case letters without ascenders and descenders, as measured from the base line to the top of the face of the lower case x

Bibliography

1	Alderman E	1938	The effect of size of type on speed of reading and the determination of various factors that may influence the results	The Pittsburgh Schools 13 (November/December), pp.33-63
2	Anderson IH and Meredith CW	1948	The reading of projected books with special reference to rate and visual fatigue	Journal of Educational Research 41 (February), pp.453-60
3	Anderson NS Braunstein M and Novick L	1960	An evaluation of human readability and recognition of a specialized font	IBM Research Center Report No. RC-219
4	Andrews RB	1949	Reading power unlimited	Texas Outlook 33, pp.20-1
5	Anthony MJ	1949	Just the type: a manual on improved typography for newspaper advertising	Danville, Illinois: Newspaper Advertising Executives Association
6	Atkinson WH Crumley LM and Willis MP	1952	A study of the requirements for letters, numbers, and markings to be used on trans-illuminated aircraft control panels. Part 5: The comparative legibility of three fonts for numerals	US Naval Air Material Centre Report TED No. NAM EL-609
7	Baird JW	1917	The legibility of a telephone directory	Journal of Applied Psychology 1 (March),pp.30-7
8	Banister H	1927	Block capital letters as tests of visual acuity	British Journal of Ophthalmology 11, pp.49-61
9	Banister H Hartridge H and Lythgoe RJ	1927	The influence of illumination on visual acuity	British Journal of Ophthalmology 11, pp.321-30
10	Bayer H	1967	Herbert Bayer: painter, designer, architect	New York: Reinhold
11	Bayle E	1942	The nature and causes of regressive movements in reading	J. Exp. Educ. 11, pp.16-36
12	Bell HM	1939	The comparative legibility of typewriting, manuscript and cursive script. I. Easy prose, letters, and syllables	Journal of Psychology 8 (October), pp.295-309
13	Bell HM	1939	The comparative legibility of typewriting, manuscript, and cursive script. II. Difficult prose and eye-movement photography	Journal of Psychology 8 (October), pp.311-20
14	Bentley M	1921	Leading and legibility	Psychological Monographs 30, pp.48-61
15	Berger C	1944	Stroke-width, form and horizontal spacing of numerals as determinants of the threshold of recognition. Part I	Journal of Applied Psychology 28 (June), pp.208-31
16	Berger C	1944	Stroke width, form and horizontal spacing of numerals as determinants of the threshold of recognition. Part II	Journal of Applied Psychology 28 (August), pp.336-46
17	Berger C	1948	Some experiments on the width of symbols as determinant of legibility	Acta Ophthalmologica 26, pp.517-50
18	Berger C	1950	Experiments on the legibility of symbols of different width and height	Acta Ophthalmologica 28, pp.423-34

19	Berger C	1952	The influence of stroke-width upon the legibility (threshold of recognition) of some narrow numerals of varying height	Acta Ophthalmologica 30, pp.409-20
20	Berger C	1956	Grouping, number, and spacing of letters as determinants of word recognition	Journal of General Psychology 55 (October), pp.215-28
21	Bergh G van den	1958	Capital letters, twin- and multiple-print	Haarlem: H.D. Tjeenk Willink & Zoon
22	Berliner A	1920	Atmosphärenwert von Drucktypen	Z.angew.Psych 17, p.165
23	Betts EA	1942	A study of paper as a factor in type visibility	Optometric Weekly 33 (April 9), pp.229-32
24	Bitterman ME	1945	Electromyographic recording of eyelid movements	American Journal of Psychology 58 (January), pp.112-3
25	Bitterman ME	1945	Heart rate and frequency of blinking as indices of visual efficiency	Journal of Experimental Psychology 35 (August), pp.279-92
26	Bitterman ME	1946	A Reply to Dr Luckiesh	Journal of Experimental Psychology 36 (April), pp.182-4
27	Bitterman ME and Soloway E	1946	The relation between frequency of blinking and effort expended in mental work	Journal of Experimental Psychology 36 (April), pp.134-6
28	Bitterman ME and Soloway E	1946	Minor studies from the Psychological Laboratory of Cornell University, XCIII. Frequency of blinking as a measure of visual efficiency: some methodological considerations	American Journal of Psychology 59 (October), pp.676-81
29	Blackhurst JH	1921	The typography of elementary school readers	School and Society 14 (November 5), pp.407-8
30	Blackhurst JH	1922	Size of type as related to readability in the first four grades	School and Society 16, pp.697-700
31	Blackhurst JH	1923	Leading as related to readability in the first four grades	School and Society 17, pp.363-4
32	Blackhurst JH	1923	Length of line as related to readability in the first four grades	School and Society 18, pp.328-30
33	Blackhurst JH	1927	Investigations in the hygiene of reading	Baltimore: Warwick and York
34	Blackhurst JH	1928	Hygienic standards in type and format of reading materials	Elementary English Review 5 (April), pp.101-3, 118
35	Bowerman CW (Chairman)	1922	Report of the Committee appointed to select the best faces of type and modes of display for government printing	London: HM Stationery Office Reviewed in the British Journal of Ophthalmology 6 (October), pp.475-9
36	Breland K and Breland MK	1944	Legibility of newspaper headlines printed in capitals and lower case	Journal of Applied Psychology 28 (April), pp.117-20
37	Bridgman CS and Wade EA	1956	Optimum letter size for a given display area	Journal of Applied Psychology 40 (December), pp.378-80
38	British Association for the Advancement of Science	1913	Report on the influence of school books on eye-sight	London: Murrary

39	Brown F R	1953	A study of the requirements for letters, numbers and markings to be used on trans-illuminated aircraft control panels, Part 4. Legibility of uniform stroke capital letters as determined by size and height to width ratio and as compared to Garamond Bold.	US Naval Air Material Center Report TED No. NAM EL-609 Part 4
40	Brown F R and Lowery EA	1949	A study of the requirements for letters, numbers and markings to be used on trans-illuminated aircraft control panels. Part 1. The effects of stroke width upon the legibility of capital letters	US Naval Air Material Center Report TED No. NAM EL-609 Part 1
41	Brown F R and Lowery EA	1950	A study of the requirements for letters, numbers and markings to be used on trans-illuminated aircraft control panels. Part 2. A survey of pilot preferences for markings for rheostat controls	US Naval Air Material Center Report TED No. NAM EL-609 Part 2
42	Brown F R Lowery EA and Willis MP	1951	A study of the requirements for letters, numbers and markings to be used on trans-illuminated aircraft control panels. Part 3. The effect of stroke width and form upon the legibility of numerals	US Naval Air Material Center Report TED No. NAM EL-609 Part 3
43	Brown WC et al	1952	American standard practice for industrial lighting	New York: Illuminating Engineering Society
44	Bryan AI	1945	Legibility of Library of Congress cards and their reproductions	College and Research Libraries 6, pp.447-64
45	Buckingham BR	1931	New data on the typography of text-books	Yearbook of the National Society for the Study of Education 30, pp.93-125
46	Buckingham BR	1933	Type sizes of first-grade textbooks are tested for readability	Nation's Schools 12 (September), pp.45-8
47	Burt C	1959	A psychological study of typography	London: Cambridge University Press
48	Burt C	1960	The typography of children's books - a record of research in the UK	Yearbook of Education pp.242-56
49	Burt C Cooper WF and Martin JL	1955	A psychological study of typography	British Journal of Statistical Psychology 8, pp.29-57
50	Burtt HE	1938	Psychology of Advertising Chapter XVII: Typography	Boston: Houghton Mifflin Co
51	Burtt HE	1949	Typography and readability	Elementary English 26 (April), pp.212-21
52	Burtt HE and Basch C	1923	Legibility of Bodoni, Baskerville Roman, and Cheltenham type faces	Journal of Applied Psychology 7 (September), pp.237-45
53	Burtt HE Beck HC and Campbell E	1928	Legibility of backbone titles	Journal of Applied Psychology 12 (April), pp.217-27

54	Carlson TR	1949	The relationship between speed and accuracy of comprehension	Journal of Educational Research 42, pp.500-12
55	Carmichael L and Dearborn WF	1947	Reading and visual fatigue	Boston: Houghton Mifflin Co
56	Cattell J McK	1885	The inertia of the eye and brain	Brain 8 (October), pp.295-313
57	Cattell J McK	1885	Über die Zeit der Erkennung und Benennung von Schriftzeichen, Bildern und Farben	Phil. Stud. 2, pp.635-50
58	Chang CY	1942	A study of the relative merits of vertical and horizontal lines in reading Chinese print	Arch Psych 276
59	Cheetham D and Grimbly B	1964	Design analysis: Type face	Design 186 pp.61-71
60	Cheetham D Poulton EC and Grimbly B	1965	The case for research	Design 195 pp.48-51
61	Chou En-Lai et al	1958	Reform of the Chinese written language	Peking: Foreign Languages Press
62	Chou SK	1929	Reading and legibility of Chinese characters	Journal of Experimental Psychology 12, pp.156-77
63	Clark B and Wavern N	1940	A photographic study of reading during a 65 hour vigil	Journal of Educational Psychology 31, pp.383-90
64	Cohn HL	1886	Hygiene of the eye in schools	London: Simpkin & Marshall
65	Cohn HL and Rübencamp R	1903	Wie sollen Bücher und Zeitungen gedruckt werden	Brunswick: Vieweg & Sohn
66	Coleman EB and Hahn SC	1966	Failure to improve readability with a vertical typography	Journal of Applied Psychology 50, pp.434-6
67	Coleman EB and Kim I	1961	Comparison of several styles of typography in English	Journal of Applied Psychology 45, pp.262-7
68	Cornog DY Rose FC and Walkowicz JL	1964	Legibility of alphanumeric characters and other symbols I. A permutated title index and bibliography	NBS Misc. Publ. 262-1 US Department of Commerce
69	Cornog DY and Rose FC	1967	Legibility of alphanumeric characters and other symbols II. A reference handbook	NBS Misc. Publ. 262-2 US Department of Commerce
70	Crook MN and Baxter FS	1954	The design of digits	USAF WADC Technical Report 54-262
71	Crook MN Hanson JA and Weisz A	1954	Legibility of type as a function of stroke width, letter width and letter spacing under low illumination	USAF WADC Technical Report 53-440
72	Crook MN Hanson JA and Weisz A	1954	Legibility of type as determined by the combined effect of typographical variables and reflectance of background	USAF WADC Technical Report 53-441
73	Crook MN Hanson JA and Wulfeck JW	1952	The legibility of type as a function of reflectance of background under low illumination	USAF WADC Technical Report 52-85

74	Crook MN Hoffman AC and Wessell NY	1947	Effect of vibration on the legibility of numerical material	American Psychologist 2, pp.347-8
75	Crosland H	1929	The influence of letter position on range of apprehension - a reply to Dr Tinker	Psychological Bulletin 26, pp.375-7
76	Crosland H and Johnson G	1928	The range of apprehension as affected by inter-letter hair-spacing and by characteristics of individual letters	Journal of Applied Psychology 12 (February), pp.82-124
77	Crouwel W	1967	Proposal for a new alphabet	Hilversum: de Jong & Co
78	Dair C	1967	Design with type	University of Toronto Press
79	Dearborn WF	1906	The psychology of reading: Chapter XII. The length of text-lines and motor habits	Archives of Philosophy, Psychology and Scientific Methods 4
80	Dearborn WF and Anderson IH	1937	A new method for teaching phrasing and for increasing the size of reading fixations	Psychological Record 1, pp.459-75
81	Dearborn WF Johnston PW and Carmichael L	1949	Oral stress and meaning in printed material	Science 110, p.404
82	Dearborn WF Johnston PW and Carmichael L	1951	Improving the readability of typewritten manuscripts	Proceedings of the National Academy of Sciences 37, (October), pp.670-2
83	Didelot M	1931	What type sizes and measures offer the maximum legibility?	Inland Printer 88 (December), pp.35-7
84	Dixon JC	1948	Effect of exposure-time on perception of grouped digits	American Journal of Psychology 61 (July), pp.396-9
85	Dockeray FC	1910	The span of vision in reading and the legibility of letters	Journal of Educational Psychology 1, pp.123-31
86	Dodge R	1900	Visual perception during eye movements	The Psychological Review 7, pp.454-65
87	Dodge R	1905	The illusion of clear vision during eye movements	Psychological Bulletin 2, pp.193-9
88	Dolch EW	1949	Phrase perception in reading	Elementary School Journal 49, pp.341-7
89	Dowding G	1957	Factors in the choice of type faces	London: Wace & Co
90	Downing J	1968	Reform of the English writing-system	The Penrose Annual 61, pp.102-6
91	Durkee B	1940	Design for legibility	Sixth Graphic Arts Production Yearbook p.331
92	ECMA	1965	ECMA standard for the alphanumeric character set OCR-B for optical recognition (ECMA 11)	Geneva: European Computer Manufacturers Association
93	English E	1944	A study of the readability of four newspaper headline types	Journalism Quarterly 21 (September), pp.217-29
94	Erdmann B and Dodge R	1898	Psychologische Untersuchungen über das Lesen, auf experimenteller Grundlage	Halle: Max Niemeyer
95	Ewing AE	1922	The value of letters and characters in visual tests	International Congress of Opthalmology pp.604-6

89

96	Fabrizio R Kaplan I and Teal G	1967	Readability as a function of the straightness of right-hand margins	Journal of Typographic Research 1, pp.90-5
97	Finzi J	1900	Zur Untersuchung der Auffassungsfähigkeit und Merkfähigkeit	Psychologische Arbeiten 3, pp.289-384
98	Fishenden RB	1946	Types, paper and printing in relation to eye strain	British Journal of Ophthalmology 30, pp.20-6
99	Fisher P	1954	History of type readability studies discloses no 'perfect' type face	Inland Printer (June), pp.66-7
100	Flores I	1960	Methods for comparing the legibility of printed numerals	Journal of Psychology 50 (July), pp.3-14
101	Forbes TW Moscowitz K and Morgan G	1951	A comparison of lower case and capital letters for highway signs	In Proceedings of the 30th Annual Meeting, pp.355-73 Washington, DC: Highway Research Board National Research Council
102	Foster JJ	1966	A review of psychological research on the legibility of print	Manchester College of Art and Design
103	Fox JG	1963	A comparison of Gothic elite and standard elite type faces	Ergonomics 6, pp.193-8
104	Frutiger A	1967	OCR-B: a standardized character for optical recognition	Typographische Monatsblatter (January)
105	Gage HL	1937	Research in readability: 1. The program for research	Linotype News 16 (September), p.2.
106	Gage HL	1938	Research in readability: 2. Effects of leading	Linotype News 16 (March), p.2.
107	Gage HL	1946	What makes type readable?	Linotype Bulletin 327, p.235
108	Gates AI	1931	What do we know about optimum lengths of lines in reading	Journal of Educational Research 23, pp.1-7
109	Gill E	1931	An Essay on Typography	London: Sheed & Ward
110	Gilliland AR	1923	The effect on reading of changes in the size of type	Elementary School Journal 24 (October), pp.138-46
111	Glanville AD Kreezer GL and Dallenbach KM	1946	The effect of type-size on accuracy of apprehension and speed of localising words	American Journal of Psychology, 59 (April), pp.220-35
112	Goldscheider A and Müller RF	1893	Zur Physiologie und Pathologie des Lesens	Zeitschr.f.Klin. Med. 23, p.131
113	Gould PN Raines LC and Rucknick CA	1921	The printing of backbone titles on thin books and magazines	Psychological Monographs 30, pp.62-76
114	Gray WS	1925	Summary of investigations relating to reading	Supplementary Educational Monographs 82
115	Greene EB	1933	The legibility of typewritten material	Journal of Applied Psychology 17 (December), pp.713-28
116	Greene EB	1934	The relative legibility of linotyped and typewritten material	Journal of Applied Psychology 18, pp.697-704

117	Gregory RL	1966	Eye and Brain: the psychology of seeing	London: Weidenfeld and Nicolson
118	Griffing H and Franz SI	1896	On the Condition of Fatigue in Reading	Psychological Review 3 (September), pp.513-30
119	Hackman RB and Tinker MA	1957	Effect of variations in color of print and background upon eye movements in reading	American Journal of Optometry 34 (July), pp.354-9
120	Hailstone M and Foster JJ	1967	Studies of the efficiency of drug labelling	Manchester College of Art and Design
121	Hartridge H and Owen HB	1922	Test types	British Journal of Ophthalmology 6, pp.543-9
122	Haskins JB	1958	Testing the suitability of type-faces for editorial subject matter	Journalism Quarterly 35, pp.186-94
123	Hewitt G	1943	Pen to Pantograph	London School of Printing
124	Hodge DC	1962	Legibility of a uniform stroke-width alphabet: I. Relative legibility of upper and lower case letters	Journal of Engineering Psychology 1 (January), pp.34-46
125	Hodge DC	1963	Legibility of a uniform stroke-width alphabet: II. Some factors affecting the legibility of words	Journal of Engineering Psychology, 2 (April), pp.55-67
126	Hoffman AC	1946	Eye movements during prolonged reading	Journal of Experimental Psychology 36 (April) 95-118
127	Hoffman AC Wellman B and Carmichael L	1939	A quantitative comparison of the electrical and photographic techniques of eye-movement recording	Journal of Experimental Psychology 24 (January), pp.40-53
128	Hollingworth HL	1920	Advertising and Selling	New York: D. Appleton & Co
129	Holmes G	1931	The relative legibility of black print and white print	Journal of Applied Psychology 15 (June), pp.248-51
130	Horton DL and Mecherikoff M	1960	Letter preferences: ranking the alphabet	Journal of Applied Psychology 44 (August), pp.252-3
131	Hovde HT	1929	The relative effect of size of type, leading and context, Part I	Journal of Applied Psychology 13 (December), pp.600-29
132	Hovde HT	1930	The relative effect of size of type, leading and context, Part II	Journal of Applied Psychology 14 (February), pp.63-73
133	Howell WC and Kraft CL	1961	The judgement of size, contrast, and sharpness of letter forms	Journal of Experimental Psychology 61 (January), pp.30-9
134	Huey EB	1898	Preliminary experiments in the physiology and psychology of reading	American Journal of Psychology 9 (July), pp.375-86
135	Huey EB	1908	The psychology and pedagogy of reading	New York: The Macmillan Co.
136	Hughes CL	1961	Variability of stroke width within digits	Journal of Applied Psychology 45, pp.364-9
137	Hurd F	1947	Glance legibility	Traffic Engineering 17 (January), pp.161-2

138	Hvistendahl JK	1961	Headline readability measured in context	Journalism Quarterly 38, pp.226-8
139	Institute for Applied Experimental Psychology	1952	Legibility of printed material Section II, Chapter IV, Part III of handbook of human engineering data	Special Devices Center Human Engineering Technical report SDC 199-1-2a
140	Jastak J	1934	Interferences in reading	Psych Bull. 31, pp.244-72
141	Javal E	1878	Hygiène de la lecture	Bulletin de la Société de médécine publique, p.569
142	Javal E	1881	L'évolution de la typographie considéré dans ses rapports avec l'hygiène de la vue	Revue scientifique 27, pp.802-13
143	Javal E	1905	Physiologie de la lecture et de l'écriture	Paris: Felix Alcan
144	Johnston E	1906	Writing and Illuminating and Lettering	London: John Hogg
145	Judd CH and Buswell GT	1922	Silent reading, a study of various types	Supplementary Educational Monographs 23
146	Kahler WH et al	1953	Recommended practice for supplementary lighting	New York: Illuminating Engineering Society
147	Ketch JM et al	1950	Recommended practice of library lighting	New York: Illuminating Engineering Society
148	Kimura D	1959	The effect of letter position on recognition	Canadian Journal of Psychology 31 (March), pp.1-10
149	Kindersley D	1966	An essay in optical letter spacing and its mechanical application	London: The Wynkyn de Worde Society
150	Kirsch R	1920	Sehschärfenuntersuchungen mit Hilfe des Visometers von Zeiss (Zugleich ein Breitrag zur frage der Lesbarkeit von Druckschriften)	Graefe's Archiv für Ophthalmologie 103 (December), pp.253-79
151	Kirschmann A	1908	Über die Erkennbarkeit geometrischer Figuren und Schriftzeichen im indirekten Sehen	Archiv für die Gesamte Psychologie 13 (December), pp.352-88
152	Kirschmann A	1916	Antiqua oder Fraktur (3rd Ed.)	Leipzig: Deutscher Buchgewerbeverein
153	Klare GR	1963	The measurement of readability	Ames: Iowa State University Press
154	Klare GR Mabry JE and Gustafson LM	1955	Relationship of style difficulty to immediate retention and to acceptability of technical material	Journal of Educational Psychology 46, pp.287-95
155	Klare GR Mabry JE and Gustafson LM	1955	The relationship of patterning (underlining) to immediate retention and to acceptability of technical material	Journal of Applied Psychology 39, pp.40-2
156	Klare GR Mabry JE and Gustafson LM	1955	Relationship of human interest to immediate retention and to acceptability of technical material	Journal of Applied Psychology 39, pp.92-5
157	Klare GR Nichols WH and Shuford EH	1957	The relationship of typographic arrangement to the learning of technical training material	Journal of Applied Psychology 41 (February), pp.41-5

158	Klare GR Shuford EH and Nichols WH	1957	Relationship of style difficulty, practice and ability to efficiency of reading and retention	Journal of Applied Psychology 41, pp.222-6
159	Klare GR Shuford EH and Nichols WH	1958	The relation of format organisation to learning	Educational Research Bulletin 37, pp.39-45
160	Koopman HL	1909	Scientific tests of types	Printing Art 13,pp.81-3
161	Koopman HL	1909	Types and eyes	Printing Art 12,pp.359-61
162	Korte W	1923	Über die Gestaltauffassung im indirekten sehen	Z. Psychol. 93, pp.17-83
163	Kujus H	1955	Schrift und Auge	Klin. Monatsblätter für Augenheilk 126, pp.220-9
164	Kuntz JE and Sleight RB	1949	Effect of target brightness on 'normal' and 'subnormal' visual acuity	Journal of Applied Psychology 33 (February), pp.83-91
165	Kuntz JE and Sleight RB	1950	Legibility of numerals: the optimal ratio of height to width of stroke	American Journal of Psychology 63 (October), pp.567-75
166	La Grone CW	1942	An experimental study of the relationship of peripheral perception to factors in reading	J Exp Educ. 11, pp.37-49
167	Landsell H	1954	Effect of form on the legibility of numbers	Canadian Journal of Psychology 8 (June), pp.77-9
168	Lauer AR	1948	Certain structural components of letters for improving the efficiency of the stop sign	In Proceedings of the 27th Annual Meeting, pp.360-71 Washington, DC: Highway Research Board National Research Council
169	Lauer AR and Stone JA	1955	Legibility distance and visibility distance	Optometric Weekly 46 (May), pp.727-8
170	Lawe FW	1927	The technique of reading	J Nat Instit Indus. Psych 3, pp.364-7
171	Lawson	1959	Scientific attempts to study legibility	Inland American Printer 144 No. 1
172	Legros LA	1922	A note on the legibility of printed matter	London: HM Stationery Office
173	Legros LA and Grant JC	1916	Typographical printing surfaces	London: Longmans, Green & Co.
174	Letson CT	1958	Speed and comprehension in reading	Journal of Educational Research 52, pp.49-53
175	Letson CT	1959	The relative influence of material and purpose on reading rates	Journal of Educational Research 52, pp.238-40
176	Linotype Matrix	1956	Legibility where it matters	London: Linotype & Machinery No.26 (December),p.6
177	Luckiesh M	1923	Light and color in advertising and merchandising Chapter XIV: Electrical Advertising	New York: D van Nostrand
178	Luckiesh M	1937	The perfect reading page	Electrical Engineering 56 (July), pp.779-81

179	Luckiesh M	1944	Light, vision and seeing	New York: D van Nostrand
180	Luckiesh M	1946	Discussion: Comments on criteria of ease of reading	Journal of Experimental Psychology 36 (April), pp.180-2
181	Luckiesh M	1947	Reading and the rate of blinking	Journal of Experimental Psychology 37, pp.266-8
182	Luckiesh M and Moss F K	1935	The effect of visual effort upon the heart-rate	Journal of General Psychology 13 (July), pp.131-9
183	Luckiesh M and Moss F K	1935	Visibility: its measurement and significance in seeing	Journal of the Franklin Inst. 220, pp.431-66
184	Luckiesh M and Moss F K	1935	The relative visibility of print in terms of illumination intensity	Sight-Saving Review 5 (December), pp.272-80
185	Luckiesh M and Moss F K	1937	The science of seeing	New York: D van Nostrand
186	Luckiesh M and Moss F K	1937	The visibility of various type faces	Journal of the Franklin Inst. 223 (January), pp.77-82
187	Luckiesh M and Moss F K	1937	The eyelid reflex as a criterion of ocular fatigue	Journal of Experimental Psychology 20 (June), pp.589-96
188	Luckiesh M and Moss F K	1938	Effects of leading on readability	Journal of Applied Psychology 22 (April), pp.140-60
189	Luckiesh M and Moss F K	1938	Visibility and readability of print on white and tinted papers	Sight-Saving Review 8 (June), pp.123-34
190	Luckiesh M and Moss F K	1939	The quantitative relationship between visibility and type size	Journal of the Franklin Institute 227 (January), pp.87-97
191	Luckiesh M and Moss F K	1939	The visibility and readability of printed matter	Journal of Applied Psychology 23 (December), pp.645-59
192	Luckiesh M and Moss F K	1939	Frequency of blinking as a clinical criterion of ease of seeing	American Journal of Ophthalmology 22 (June), pp.616-21
193	Luckiesh M and Moss F K	1939	Brightness-contrasts in seeing	Trans. Illuminating Engineering Society 34, pp.571-97
194	Luckiesh M and Moss F K	1939	The readability of stencil-duplicated materials	Sight-Saving Review 9 (December), pp.295-304
195	Luckiesh M and Moss F K	1940	Boldness as a factor in type-design and typography	Journal of Applied Psychology 24 (April), pp.170-83
196	Luckiesh M and Moss F K	1940	Criteria of readability	Journal of Experimental Psychology 27 (September), pp.256-70
197	Luckiesh M and Moss F K	1940	A summary of researches involving blink rate as a criterion of ease of seeing	Trans. Illuminating Engineering Society 35, pp.19-32
198	Luckiesh M and Moss F K	1941	The effect of line length on readability	Journal of Applied Psychology 25 (February), pp.67-75
199	Luckiesh M and Moss F K	1941	The visibility of print on various qualities of paper	Journal of Applied Psychology 25 (April), pp.152-8
200	Luckiesh M and Moss F K	1941	The variation in visual acuity with fixation-distance	Journal of the Optical Society of America 31 (September), pp.594-5

201	Luckiesh M and Moss F K	1941	The extent of the perceptual span in reading	Journal of General Psychology 25 (October), pp.267-72
202	Luckiesh M and Moss F K	1941	Visibility and seeing	Journal of the Franklin Institute 231, pp.323-43
203	Luckiesh M and Moss F K	1942	Reading as a visual task	New York: D van Nostrand
204	Luckiesh M and Moss F K	1942	The task of reading	Elementary School Journal 42, pp.510-4
205	Luckiesh M and Moss F K	1942	Visual tasks in comic books	Sight-Saving Review 12 (March), pp.19-24
206	Luckiesh M and Moss F K	1943	Effects of astigmatism on the visibility of print	American Journal of Ophthalmology 26 (February), pp.155-7
207	Luckiesh M and Moss F K	1943	The readability of stencil duplicated materials	Visual Digest 7, pp.26-30
208	Lyon OC	1924	The telephone directory	The Bell Telephone Quarterly 3 (July), pp.175-85
209	Lythgoe RJ	1926	Illumination and visual capacities	London: HM Stationery Office
210	Marks MB	1966	Improve reading through better format	Journal of Educational Research 60, pp.147-51
211	Mecherikoff M and Horton DL	1959	Preferences for letters of the alphabet	Journal of Applied Psychology 43 (April), pp.114-6
212	Melville JR	1957	Word-length as a factor in differential recognition	American Journal of Psychology 70 (June), pp.316-8
213	Menon TKN and Patel AS	1951	Relation of reading to comprehension	Indian J Psych 26, pp.43-53
214	Mergenthaler Linotype Company	1935	The legibility of type	Brooklyn: Mergenthaler Linotype Company
215	Mergenthaler Linotype Company	1947	The readability of type	Brooklyn: Mergenthaler Linotype Company
216	Mergenthaler Linotype Company	1947	Researches in Readability	Brooklyn: Merganthaler Linotype Company
217	Messmer O	1903	Zur Psychologie des Lesens bei Kindern und Erwachsenen	Arch f.d. ges Psychol. 2, pp.190-298
218	Millington J	1883	Are we to read backwards?	London: Field & Tuer
219	Milne JR	1915	The arrangement of mathematical tables	London: Longmans, Green & Co Napier Tercentenary Memorial Volume pp.293-316
220	Miyake R Dunlap JW and Cureton EE	1930	The comparative legibility of black and colored numbers on colored and black backgrounds	Journal of General Psychology 3 (April), pp.340-3
221	Moede W	1932	Welche Schrift ist leichter lesbar?	Frankfurt/M: Bauersche Giesserei Futuraheft 1931/32

95

222	Moore JE	1939	Sex differences in speed of reading	J Exp Educ. 8, pp.110-4 and see J Exp Educ. 8, p.245 for correction
223	Morison S	1951	First principles of typography	London: Cambridge University Press
224	Mosley J	1965	The Nymph and the Grot: the revival of the sanserif letter	Typographica 12, pp.2-19
225	McClusky HY	1934	An experiment on the influence of preliminary skimming in reading	Journal of Educational Psychology 25, pp.521-9
226	McFarland RA Holway AH and Hurvick LM	1942	Studies of visual fatigue Part V: Ordinary blinking and visual fatigue	Boston: Graduate School of Business Administration Harvard University
227	McIntosh A	1965	Typewriter composition and standardisation in information printing	Printing Technology 9, I (July), pp.51-74
228	McNally HJ	1943	The readability of certain type sizes and forms in sight-saving classes	New York: Teachers College Columbia University (contribution to Education No.883)
229	McNamara WJ Paterson DG and Tinker MA	1953	The influence of size of type on speed of reading in the primary grades	Sight-Saving Review 23, pp.28-33
230	Nahinsky ID	1956	The influence of certain typographical arrangements upon the span of visual comprehension	Journal of Applied Psychology 40 (February), pp.37-9
231	Neidhart JJ et al	1960	Recommended practice for office lighting	New York: Illuminating Engineering Society
232	Nelson LP	1949	Employee handbook printing practices	Minneapolis: Industrial Relations Center University of Minnesota
233	Nerdinger E	1954	Buchstabenbuch	Munich: Callwey
234	Newland TE	1930	A study of the specific illegibilities found in the writing of Arabic numerals	Journal of Educational Research 21 (March), pp.177-85
235	Newland TE	1932	An analytical study of the development of illegibilities in handwriting from the lower grades to adulthood	Journal of Educational Research 26 (December), pp.249-58
236	North J and Jenkins LB	1951	Reading speed and comprehension as a function of typography	Journal of Applied Psychology 35 (August), pp.225-8
237	Otto HJ and Flournoy J	1956	Printed Materials (Instructional Materials Ch 1)	Rev. Educ Res. 26, pp.115-24
238	Ovink GW	1938	Legibility, atmosphere-value, and forms of printing types	Leiden: AW Sijthoff's Uitgeversmaatschappij
239	Paterson DG and Tinker MA	1929	Studies of typographical factors influencing speed of reading. II. Size of type	Journal of Applied Psychology 13 (April), pp.120-30
240	Paterson DG and Tinker MA	1930	Time-limit versus work-limit methods	American Journal of Psychology 42 (January), pp.101-4

241	Paterson DG and Tinker MA	1930	Studies of typographical factors influencing speed of reading: IV. Effect of practice on equivalence of test forms	Journal of Applied Psychology 14 (June), pp.211-7
242	Paterson DG and Tinker MA	1931	Studies of typographical factors influencing speed of reading: VI. Black type versus white type	Journal of Applied Psychology 15 (June), pp.241-7
243	Paterson DG and Tinker MA	1932	Studies of typographical factors influencing speed of reading: VIII. Space between lines or leading	Journal of Applied Psychology 16 (August), pp.388-97
244	Paterson DG and Tinker MA	1932	Studies of typographical factors influencing speed of reading: X. Style of type face	Journal of Applied Psychology 16 (December), pp.605-13
245	Paterson DG and Tinker MA	1936	Studies of typographical factors influencing speed of reading: XII. Printing surface	Journal of Applied Psychology 20 (February), pp.128-31
246	Paterson DG and Tinker MA	1938	The part-whole proportion illusion in printing	Journal of Applied Psychology 22 (August), pp.421-5
247	Paterson DG and Tinker MA	1940	Influence of line width on eye movements	Journal of Experimental Psychology 27 (November), pp.572-7
248	Paterson DG and Tinker MA	1940	How to make type readable	New York: Harper
249	Paterson DG and Tinker MA	1941	Eye movements in reading a modern type face and Old English	American Journal of Psychology 54 (January), pp.113-4
250	Paterson DG and Tinker MA	1941	Capitals versus lower case in headlines	Editor and Publisher 75, p.51
251	Paterson DG and Tinker MA	1942	Influence of size of type on eye movements	Journal of Applied Psychology 26 (April), pp.227-30
252	Paterson DG and Tinker MA	1942	Influence of line width on eye movements for six point type	Journal of Educational Psychology 33 (October), pp.552-5
253	Paterson DG and Tinker MA	1943	Eye movements in reading type sizes in optimal line widths	Journal of Experimental Psychology (December), pp.547-51
254	Paterson DG and Tinker MA	1944	Eye movements in reading optimal and non-optimal typography	Journal of Experimental Psychology 34 (February), pp.80-3
255	Paterson DG and Tinker MA	1944	Eye movements in reading black print on a white background and red print on a green background	American Journal of Psychology 57, pp.93-4
256	Paterson DG and Tinker MA	1946	Readability of newspaper headlines in capitals and lower case	Journal of Applied Psychology 30 (April), pp.161-8
257	Paterson DG and Tinker MA	1946	The relative readability of newsprint and book print	Journal of Applied Psychology 30 (October), pp.454-9
258	Paterson DG and Tinker MA	1947	Influence of leading upon the readability of newspaper type	Journal of Applied Psychology 31 (April), pp.160-3
259	Paterson DG and Tinker MA	1947	The effect of typography upon the perceptual span in reading	American Journal of Psychology 60 (July), pp.388-96
260	Payne DE	1967	Readability of typewritten material: proportional versus standard spacing	Journal of Typographic Research 1, pp.125-36

97

261	Peignot J	1967	De l'écriture à la typographie	Paris: Gallimard
262	Perry DK	1952	Speed and accuracy of reading Arabic and Roman numerals	Journal of Applied Psychology 36 (October), pp.346-7
263	Piggott R	1964	National Roman	Alphabet 1, pp.95-100
264	Pillsbury WB	1897	A study in apperception	American Journal of Psychology 8, pp.315-96
265	Pintner I	1913	Inner speech during silent reading	Psychological Review 20. pp.129-53
266	Pitman J	1964	i/t/a	Toronto: Society of Typographic Designers of Canada Format 1, pp.6-9
267	Poffenberger AT and Franken RB	1923	Appropriateness of type faces	Journal of Applied Psychology 7, pp.312-29
268	Poulton EC	1958	On reading and visual fatigue	American Journal of Psychology 71, pp.609-11
269	Poulton EC	1959	Effects of printing types and formats on the comprehension of scientific journals	MRC Applied Psychology Research Unit Report No. 346. A condensed version of this report in Nature 184 (December 5), pp.1824-5
270	Poulton EC	1960	A note on printing to make comprehension easier	Ergonomics 3 (July), pp.245-8
271	Poulton EC	1964	Identifying the names and dosage of drugs	J. Pharm. Pharmacol. 16, pp.213-9
272	Poulton EC	1965	Letter differentiation and rate of comprehension in reading	Journal of Applied Psychology 49, pp.358-62
273	Powers SP	1962	The effect of three typesetting styles on the speed of reading newspaper content	MA Thesis University of Florida School of Journalism & Communications
274	Pratt CC	1924	A note on the legibility of items in a bibliography	Journal of Applied Psychology 8, pp.362-4
275	Pressey, LC and Pressey SL	1927	Analysis of three thousand illegibilities in the handwriting of children and of adults	Educational Research Bulletin 6 (September), pp.270-3, 285
276	Preston K Schwankl HP and Tinker MA	1932	The effect of variations in color of print and background on legibility	Journal of General Psychology 6 (April), pp.459-61
277	Prince JH	1957	Relationships of reading types to uncorrectable visual acuity	American Journal of Optometry 34, pp.581-95
278	Prince JH	1960	Visual acuity & reading in relation to letter and word design	Ohio State University Institute for Research in Vision, Publication No.1
279	Prince JH	1964	Aid for the visually handicapped: a guide for printers and publishers	Ohio State University Research Center, preliminary report to the American Library Association, Chicago
280	Prince JH	1967	Printing for the visually handicapped	Journal of Typographic Research 1 (January), pp.31-47

281	Pyke RL	1926	Report on the legibility of print	London: HM Stationery Office Medical Research Council Special Report Series No. 110
282	Radojevic S	1921	Die Erkennbarkeit von Antiqua- und Frakturbuchstaben im indirecten Sehen	Archiv für Augenheilkunde 88, pp.192-7
283	Robinson FP	1933	The role of eye movements in reading with an evaluation of the techniques for their improvement	Ames: Iowa State University Prog. Res. No. 39
284	Robinson FP	1940	Speed versus comprehension in reading: a discussion	Journal of Educational Psychology 31, pp.554-8
285	Roethlein BE	1912	The relative legibility of different faces of printing types	American Journal of Psychology 23 (January), pp.1-36
286	Ruediger WC	1907	The field of distinct vision	Columbia University Archives of Psychology 5
287	Russell DH	1958	Some research on the impact of reading	English Journal 47, pp.398-413
288	Ryan TA and Schwartz CB	1956	Speed of perception as a function of mode of presentation	American Journal of Psychology 69, pp.60-9
289	Sanford EC	1888	The relative legibility of the small letters	American Journal of Psychology 1 (May), pp.402-35
290	Schapiro HB	1952	Factors affecting legibility of digits	WADC Tech Report No. 52-127
291	Schmidt WA	1917	An experimental study in the psychology of reading	Supplementary Educational Monographs 1,2
292	Scott WD	1903	The Theory of advertising Chapter VIII: Psychological Experiment (Legibility of a Time Table)	Boston: Small, Maynard & Co
293	Seibert WF Kasten DF and Potter JR	1959	A study of factors influencing the legibility of televised characters	Journal of the SMPTE 68 (July), pp.467-72
294	Shaw A	1968	Print for poor-vision readers	The Penrose Annual 61,pp.92-101
295	Shen E	1927	An analysis of eye-movements in the reading of Chinese	Journal of Experimental Psychology 10, pp.158-63
296	Shurtleff D	1966	Design problems in visual displays Part 1: Classical factors in the legibility of numerals and capital letters	Washington DC: US Department of Commerce AD 636.414
297	Simon O	1945	Introduction to typography	London: Faber and Faber
298	Skordahl DM	1958	Effect of sloping text upon the speed of reading and upon visibility	University of Minnesota: Unpublished paper
299	Soar RS	1951	Readability of typography in psychological journals	Journal of Applied Psychology 35 (February), pp.64-7
300	Soar RS	1955	Height-width proportion and stroke width in numerical visibility	Journal of Applied Psychology 39 (February), pp.43-6

301	Soar RS	1955	Stroke width, illumination level, and figure-ground contrast in numeral visibility	Journal of Applied Psychology 39 (December), pp.429-32
302	Solomon RL and Postman L	1952	Frequency of usage as a determinant of recognition thresholds for words	Journal of Experimental Psychology 43, pp.195-201
303	Spencer H	1952	Design in Business Printing	London: Sylvan Press
304	Stanton FN and Burtt HE	1935	The influence of surface and tint of paper on speed of reading	Journal of Applied Psychology 19 (December), pp.683-93
305	Starch D	1914	Advertising	New York: Scott, Foresman and Co
306	Starch D	1923	Principles of Advertising Chapter XXV: Layout and Typography	Chicago: AW Shaw Co
307	Stern B	1950	Upper versus lower case copy as a factor in typesetting speed for linotype trainees	Journal of Applied Psychology 34 (October), pp.351-4
308	Stikar J	1961	Citelnost Cislic (Legibility of numerals)	Ceskoslovenska Psychologie 5 (Fourth Quarter), pp.358-62
309	Stolurow LM and Newman J	1959	A factional analysis of objective features of printed language presumably related to reading difficulty	Journal of Educational Research 52, pp.243-51
310	Stround JB	1945	Rate of visual perception as a factor in rate of reading	Journal of Educational Psychology 36, pp.486-8
311	Sumner FC	1932	Influence of color on legibility of copy	Journal of Applied Psychology 16 (April), pp.201-4
312	Sutherland J	1946	Relationship between perceptual span and rate of reading	Journal of Educational Psychology 37, pp.378-80
313	Tannenbaum PH Jacobsen HK and Norris EL	1964	An experimental investigation of typeface connotations	Journalism Quarterly 41, pp.65-73
314	Tarr JC	1949	How to Plan Print (2nd edition)	London: Crosby Lockwood
315	Taylor CD	1933	The legibility of black and white print	Ph.D. thesis, University of Minnesota
316	Taylor CD	1934	The relative legibility of black and white print	The Journal of Educational Psychology 25 (November), pp.561-78
317	Taylor CD and Tinker MA	1932	The effect of luminosity on the apprehension of achromatic stimuli	Journal of General Psychology 6 (April), pp.456-8
318	Taylor NW	1931	On the improvement of the dictionary	Science 74 (October 9), pp.367-8
319	Terry PW	1921	The reading problem in arithmetic	Journal of Educational Psychology 12 (October), pp.365-77
320	Terry PW	1922	How numerals are read	Supplementary Educational Monographs No. 18 (June)
321	Themerson S	1965	A well-justified postscript: typographical topography	The Penrose Annual 58, pp.334-43

322	Thurstone LL	1954	The measurement of values	Psychological Review 61, pp.47-58
323	Tinker MA	1926	Reading reactions for mathematical formulae	Journal of Experimental Psychology 9 (December), pp.444-67
324	Tinker MA	1927	Legibility and eye movements in reading	Psychological Bulletin 24 (November), pp.621-39
325	Tinker MA	1928	A photographic study of eye movements in reading formulae	Genetic Psychology Monographs 3 (February), pp.95-136
326	Tinker MA	1928	Numerals versus words for efficiency in reading	Journal of Applied Psychology 12 (April), pp.190-9
327	Tinker MA	1928	How formulae are read	American Journal of Psychology 40 (July), pp.476-83
328	Tinker MA	1928	The relative legibility of the letters, the digits, and of certain mathematical signs	Journal of General Psychology 1 (July-October), pp.472-96
329	Tinker MA	1928	Eye-movement duration, pause duration and reading time	Psychological Review 35, pp.385-97
330	Tinker MA	1929	Visual apprehension and perception in reading	Psychological Bulletin 26 (April), pp.223-40
331	Tinker MA	1929	Photographic measures of reading ability	Journal of Educational Psychology 20, pp.184-91
332	Tinker MA	1930	The relative legibility of modern and old style numerals	Journal of Experimental Psychology 13 (October), pp.453-61
333	Tinker MA	1931	Apparatus for recording eye movements	American Journal of Psychology 43 (January), pp.115-8
334	Tinker MA	1931	Physiological psychology of reading	Psychological Bulletin 28 (February), pp.81-97
335	Tinker MA	1932	The effect of color on visual apprehension and perception	Genetic Psychology Monographs 11 (February), pp.61-136
336	Tinker MA	1932	The influence of form of type on the perception of words	Journal of Applied Psychology 16 (April), pp.167-74
337	Tinker MA	1932	Studies in scientific typography	Psychological Bulletin 29 (November), pp.670-1
338	Tinker MA	1932	The relation of speed to comprehension in reading	School and Society 36, pp.158-60
339	Tinker MA	1933	Use and limitations of eye movements measures of reading	Psychological Bulletin 30, p.583 (abstract)
340	Tinker MA	1934	Experimental study of reading	Psychological Bulletin 31 (February), pp.98-110
341	Tinker MA	1934	Illumination and the hygiene of reading	Journal of Educational Psychology 25 (December), pp.669-80
342	Tinker MA	1934	The reliability and validity of eye movement measures of reading	Psychological Bulletin 31, p.741 (abstract)

343	Tinker MA	1935	Cautions concerning illumination intensities used for reading	American Journal of Optometry 12 (February), pp. 43-51
344	Tinker MA	1935	The role of set in typographical studies	Journal of Applied Psychology 19, pp.647-51
345	Tinker MA	1935	Illumination intensities for reading	American Journal of Ophthalmology 18, pp.1036-9
346	Tinker MA	1936	Eye movements in reading	Journal of Educational Research 30, pp.241-77
347	Tinker MA	1936	Eye movement, perception, and legibility in reading	Psychological Bulletin 33 (April), pp.279-90
348	Tinker MA	1936	Time taken for eye movements in reading	J Genet Psych 48, pp.468-71
349	Tinker MA	1936	Reliability and validity of eye-movement measures of reading	Journal of Experimental Psychology 19 (December), pp.732-46
350	Tinker MA	1939	Illumination standards for effective and comfortable vision	Journal of Consulting Psychology 3 (January/February), pp.11-20
351	Tinker MA	1939	The effect of illumination intensities upon speed of perception and upon fatigue in reading	Journal of Educational Psychology 30 (November), pp.561-71
352	Tinker MA	1939	Speed versus comprehension in reading as affected by level of difficulty	Journal of Educational Psychology 30, pp.81-94
353	Tinker MA	1940	Dr Robinson on speed versus comprehension in reading: a discussion	Journal of Educational Psychology 31, pp.559-60
354	Tinker MA	1940	Effect of visual adaptation upon intensity of light preferred for reading	Psychological Bulletin 37, p.575 (abstract)
355	Tinker MA	1941	Effect of visual adaptation upon intensity of light preferred for reading	American Journal of Psychology 54 (October), pp.559-63
356	Tinker MA	1942	Individual and sex differences in speed of saccadic eye movements	New York: McGraw Hill pp.271-80 in Studies in Personality McNemer Q & Merril MA (eds)
357	Tinker MA	1942	The effect of adaptation upon visual efficiency in illumination studies	American Journal of Optometry 19 (April), pp.143-51
358	Tinker MA	1943	Readability of comic books	American Journal of Optometry 20 (March), pp.89-93
359	Tinker MA	1943	Illumination intensities for reading newspaper type	Journal of Educational Psychology 34 (April), pp.247-50
360	Tinker MA	1944	Criteria for determining the readability of type faces	Journal of Educational Psychology 35 (October), pp.385-96
361	Tinker MA	1944	Illumination intensities preferred for reading with direct lighting	American Journal of Ophthalmology 21

362	Tinker MA	1945	Reliability of blinking frequency employed as a measure of readability	Journal of Experimental Psychology 35 (October), pp.418-24
363	Tinker MA	1945	Effect of visual adaptation upon intensity of illumination preferred for reading with direct lighting	Journal of Applied Psychology 29 (December), pp.471-6
364	Tinker MA	1945	Rate of work in reading performance as measured in standardised tests	Journal of Educational Psychology 36, pp.217-28
365	Tinker MA	1946	The study of eye movements in reading	Psychological Bulletin 43 (March), pp.93-120
366	Tinker MA	1946	Validity of frequency of blinking as a criterion of readability	Journal of Experimental Psychology 36 (October), pp.453-60
367	Tinker MA	1946	Illumination standards	American Journal of Public Health 36, pp.963-73
368	Tinker MA	1947	Time relations for eye-movement measures in reading	Journal of Educational Psychology 38 (January), pp.1-10
369	Tinker MA	1947	Illumination standards for effective and easy seeing	Psychological Bulletin 44 (September), pp.435-50
370	Tinker MA	1948	Readability of book print and newsprint in terms of blink rate	Journal of Educational Psychology 39 (January), pp.35-39
371	Tinker MA	1948	Effect of vibration upon reading	American Journal of Psychology 61 (July), pp.386-90
372	Tinker MA	1948	Cumulative effect of marginal conditions upon rate of perception in reading	Journal of Applied Psychology 32 (October), pp.537-40
373	Tinker MA	1949	Involuntary blink rate and illumination intensity in visual work	Journal of Experimental Psychology 39 (August), pp.558-60
374	Tinker MA	1950	Reliability and validity of involuntary blinking as a measure of ease of seeing	Jounral of Educational Psychology 41 (November), pp.417-27
375	Tinker MA	1951	Fixation pause duration in reading	Journal of Educational Psychology 44 (February), pp.471-9
376	Tinker MA	1951	Derived illumination specifications	Journal of Applied Psychology 35 (December), pp.377-80
377	Tinker MA	1952	Interpretation of illumination data	American Journal of Optometry 29 (June), pp.293-300
378	Tinker MA	1952	The effect of intensity of illumination upon speed of reading six-point italic print	American Journal of Psychology 65 (October), pp.600-2
379	Tinker MA	1953	Effect of vibration upon speed of perception while reading six-point print	Journal of Educational Research 46 (February), pp.459-64
380	Tinker MA	1954	Effect of slanted text upon the readability of print	Journal of Educational Psychology 45 (May), pp.287-91
381	Tinker MA	1954	Readability of mathematical tables	Journal of Applied Psychology 38 (December), pp.436-42
382	Tinker MA	1955	Perceptual and oculomotor efficiency in reading materials in vertical and horizontal arrangements	American Journal of Psychology 68 (September), pp.444-9
383	Tinker MA	1955	Prolonged reading tasks in visual research	Journal of Applied Psychology 39 (December), pp.444-6

384	Tinker MA	1956	Effect of sloped text upon the readability of print	American Journal of Optometry 33 (April), pp.189-95
385	Tinker MA	1956	Effect of angular alignment upon readability of print	Journal of Educational Psychology 47 (October), pp.358-63
386	Tinker MA	1957	Effect of curved text upon readability of print	Journal of Applied Psychology 41 (April), pp.218-21
387	Tinker MA	1958	Effect of sloping text upon the speed of reading and upon visibility	University of Minnesota Unpublished paper
388	Tinker MA	1958	Recent studies of eye movements in reading	Psychological Bulletin 54 (July), pp.215-31
389	Tinker MA	1958	Length of work periods in visual research	Journal of Applied Psychology 42 (October), pp.343-5
390	Tinker MA	1959	Brightness contrast, illumination and visual efficiency	American Journal of Optometry 36 (May), pp.221-36
391	Tinker MA	1959	Print for children's textbooks	Education 80,No.1,pp.37-40
392	Tinker MA	1960	Legibility of mathematical tables	Journal of Applied Psychology 44 (April), pp.83-7
393	Tinker MA	1963	Legibility of print for children in the upper grades	American Journal of Optometry 40, pp.614-621
394	Tinker MA	1963	Legibility of print	Ames: Iowa State University Press
395	Tinker MA	1963	Influence of simultaneous variation in size of type, width of line and leading for newspaper type	Journal of Applied Psychology 47, pp.380-2
396	Tinker MA	1965	Bases for effective reading	Minneapolis: University of Minnesota Press
397	Tinker MA	1966	Experimental studies on the legibility of print: an annotated bibliography	Reading Research Quarterly 1, No.4 (Summer),pp.67-118
398	Tinker MA and Frandsen A	1934	Evaluation of photographic measures of reading	Journal of Educational Psychology 25 (February), pp.96-100
399	Tinker MA and Paterson DG	1928	Influence of type form on speed of reading	Journal of Applied Psychology 12 (August), pp.359-68
400	Tinker MA and Paterson DG	1929	Studies of typographical factors influencing speed of reading: III. Length of line	Journal of Applied Psychology 13 (June), pp.205-19
401	Tinker MA and Paterson DG	1931	Studies of typographical factors influencing speed of reading: V. Simultaneous variation of type size and line length	Journal of Applied Psychology 15 (February), pp.72-8
402	Tinker MA and Paterson DG	1931	Studies of typographical factors influencing speed of reading: VII. Variations in color of print and background	Journal of Applied Psychology 15 (October), pp.471-79
403	Tinker MA and Paterson DG	1932	The influence of form of type on the perception of words	Journal of Applied Psychology 16, pp.167-74

404	Tinker MA and Paterson DG	1932	Studies of typographical factors influencing speed of reading: IX. Reduction in size of newspaper print	Journal of Applied Psychology 16 (October), pp.525-31
405	Tinker MA and Paterson DG	1935	Studies of typographical factors influencing speed of reading: XI. Role of set in typographical studies	Journal of Applied Psychology 19 (December), pp.647-51
406	Tinker MA and Paterson DG	1936	Studies of typographical factors influencing speed of reading: XIII. Methodological considerations	Journal of Applied Psychology 20 (February), pp.132-45
407	Tinker MA and Paterson DG	1939	Legibility of newsprint	Psychological Bulletin 36 (October), p.634
408	Tinker MA and Paterson DG	1939	Influence of type form on eye movements	Journal of Experimental Psychology 25 (November), pp.528-31
409	Tinker MA and Paterson DG	1941	Eye movements in reading a modern type face and Old English	American Journal of Psychology 54 (January), pp.113-4
410	Tinker MA and Paterson DG	1942	Reader preferences and typography	Journal of Applied Psychology 26 (February), pp.38-40
411	Tinker MA and Paterson DG	1943	Differences among newspaper body types in readability	Journalism Quarterly 20 (June 1943), pp.152-5
412	Tinker MA and Paterson DG	1944	Eye movements in reading black print on white background and red print on dark green background	American Journal of Psychology 57 (January), pp.93-4
413	Tinker MA and Paterson DG	1944	Wartime changes in newspaper body type	Journalism Quarterly 21 (March), pp.7-11
414	Tinker MA and Paterson DG	1946	Effect of line width and leading on readability of newspaper type	Journalism Quarterly 23 (September), pp.307-9
415	Tinker MA and Paterson DG	1946	The relative readability of newsprint and book-print	Journal of Applied Psychology 30, pp.454-9
416	Tinker MA and Paterson DG	1946 '	Readability of mixed type forms	Journal of Applied Psychology 30 (December), pp.631-7
417	Tinker MA and Paterson DG	1949	Speed of reading nine point type in relation to line width and leading	Journal of Applied Psychology 33 (February), pp.81-2
418	Tinker MA and Paterson DG	1950	Typography and legibility in reading Section 9, Chapter II, in Handbook of Applied Psychology, Vol.1. Fryer DH & Henry ER (eds)	New York: Rinehart
419	Tinker MA and Paterson DG	1955	The effect of typographical variations upon eye movement in reading	Journal of Educational Research 49 (November), pp.171-84
420	Traxler AE	1932	The correlation between reading rate and comprehension	Journal of Educational Research 26, pp.97-102
421	Traxler AE	1941	Ten years of research in reading	New York: Educational Records Bureau
422	Traxler AE and Jungeblut A	1960	Research in reading during another four years	New York: Educational Records Bureau
423	Traxler AE and Townsend A	1946	Another five years of research in reading	New York: Educational Records Bureau

424	Traxler AE and Townsend A	1955	Eight more years of research in reading	New York: Educational Records Bureau
425	Tu HCT	1930	The effect of different arrangements of the Chinese language upon speed and comprehension of silent reading	J Genet Psych 38, pp.321-7
426	Turner OG	1930	The comparative legibility and speed of manuscript and cursive handwriting	Elementary School Journal 30 (June), pp.780-6
427	Uhlaner JE	1941	The effect of thickness of stroke on the legibility of letters	Proceedings of the Iowa Academy of Science 48, pp.319-24
428	Unger G	1967	A counter-proposal (to Wim Crouwel's proposal for a new alphabet)	Hilversum: de Jong & Co
429	Updike DB	1922	Printing types: their history, forms, and use	Harvard University Press
430	Vernon MD	1928	The movements of the eyes in reading	British Journal of Ophthalmology 12, pp.130-9
431	Vernon MD	1931	The experimental study of reading	London: Cambridge University Press
432	Vernon MD	1946	On the legibility of print	International Printing 1, pp.33-41
433	Vernon MD	1948	The problem of the optimum format for scientific journals. Suggestions and points for further investigation	Paper No.11 in the Royal Society Scientific Information Conference, 21 June-2 July, Report and Papers Submitted, pp.349-51
434	Vernon MD (Compiler)	1966	Visual perception and its relation to reading: an annotated bibliography	Newark, Delaware: International Reading Association
435	Vernon MD and Pickford RW	1929	Studies in the Psychology of Reading	London: HM Stationery Office
436	Warren AL	1942	The perceptibility of lower case and all capitals newspaper headlines	Master's Thesis Minnesota University
437	Webber ME et al	1953	Recommended practice for residence lighting	New York: Illuminating Engineering Society
438	Weber A	1881	Ueber die Augenuntersuchungen in den höheren Schulen in Darmstadt	
439	Weber CO	1942	Effects of practice on the perceptual span for letters	Journal of General Psychology 26, pp.347-51
440	Webster E	1963	The impact of non-impact printing	Datamation 9 (September), pp.24-30
441	Webster HA and Tinker MA	1935	The influence of type face on the legibility of print	Journal of Applied Psychology 19 (February), pp.43-52
442	Webster HA and Tinker MA	1935	The influence of paper surface on the perceptibility of print	Journal of Applied Psychology 19 (April), pp.145-7
443	Weiner J Leikind MC and Gibson JR	1952	Visibility: A bibliography	Washington, DC: Library of Congress
444	Weinland JD	1924	The effect of grouping on the perception of digits	American Journal of Psychology 35 (April), pp.222-9

445	Weiss AP	1917	The focal variator	Journal of Experimental Psychology 2 (April), pp.106-13
446	Weston HC	1935	The relation between illumination and industrial efficiency: the effect of size of work	London: HM Stationery Office
447	Weston HC	1945	The relation between illumination and visual efficiency: the effect of brightness contrast	London: HM Stationery Office
448	Weston HC	1949	Sight, light and efficiency	London: HK Lewis & Co Ltd
449	Weston HC and Taylor AK	1927	The relation between illumination and efficiency in fine work (typesetting by hand)	London: HM Stationery Office
450	Weston HC and Taylor AK	1928	The effect of different systems of lighting on output and accuracy in fine work (typesetting by hand)	London: HM Stationery Office
451	Whipple GM and Curtis JN	1917	Preliminary investigations of skimming in reading	Journal of Educational Psychology 8, pp.33-49
452	Whittemore IC	1948	What do you mean - legibility?	Print 5 (First Quarter), pp.35-7
453	Wick W	1921	Die vergleichende Bewertung der Deutschen und Lateinischen Schrift vom Standpunkt des Augenärzte	Klinische Monatsblätter für Augenheilkunde 66 (January-June), pp.758-9
454	Wiegand CF	1908	Untersuchungen über die Bedeutung der Gestaltqualität für die Erkennung von Wörtern	Zeitschr. für Psychologie und Physiol. der Sinnesorgane I, 48, pp.161-237
455	Wiggins RH	1967	Effects of three typographical variables on speed of reading	Journal of Typographic Research I, pp.5-18
456	Williamson H	1956	Methods of book design	London: Oxford University Press
457	Wood CL and Bitterman ME	1950	Blinking as a measure of effort in visual work	American Journal of Psychology 63 (October), pp.584-8
458	Woodworth RS and Schlosberg H	1954	Experimental Psychology (rev.ed.)	New York: Holt, Rinehart & Winston
459	Wrolstad ME	1960	Adult preferences in typography: exploring the function of design	Journalism Quarterly 37, pp.211-23
460	Young KD	1946	Legibility of printed materials	Engineering Division, Air Material Command Memorandum Report No. TSEAA-8-694-1A
461	Zachrisson B	1956	Some experiments with children regarding the readability of printed text	Research Bulletin No. 9 The Institute of Education University of Stockholm
462	Zachrisson B	1957	Studies in the readability of printed text with special reference to type design and type size: a survey and some contributions	Stockholm: The Graphic Institute
463	Zachrisson B	1965	Studies in the legibility of printed text	Stockholm: Almqvist & Wiksell
464	Zeitler J	1900	Tachistoskopische Versuche ueber das Lesen	Phil. Stud. 16, pp.380-463